QUICK QUIZ BOOK

A Question and Answer Reference

VOLUME 1

Questions compiled by
Stephen Vasciannie

LMH Publishing Limited

Edited by: Rose Lewis Stone

Cover Design: Susan Lee-Quee, LeeQuee Design

Book Design,Layout & Typeset by: Michelle M.A. Mitchell, PAGE Design Services

Published by: LMH Publishing Limited
7 Norman Road,
LOJ Industrial Complex
Building 10
Kingston C.S.O., Jamaica
Tel: 876-938-0005; 938-0712
Fax: 876-759-8752
Email: lmhbookpublishing@cwjamaica.com
Website: www.lmhpublishingjamaica.com

Printed in the USA   ISBN 976-8184-43-4

Acknowledgements

The questions in this book have been prepared with reference to a wide variety of sources. These are listed in the bibliography at the end of the book.

I also acknowledge, with much gratitude, the enthusiastic participation of the members of the Kingston College quiz fraternity (including various students, teachers and Old Boys). They have frequently handled some of these questions with enviable sharpness, and, more generally, have helped to consolidate the school's position as a serious contender each year in the TVJ Schools' Challenge Quiz Competition. More than anyone else, Mrs Frances Coke laid the foundation for the Kingston College tradition in Schools' Challenge activities; together with numerous other Kingston College quiz participants, I remain especially indebted to her.

Preface

This book of questions is intended to provide a supplement to traditional text-books used in secondary schools. It is based on the idea that learning is most meaningful when it is interactive: students who seek to answer a series of questions from a broad range of subject areas may find that variety encourages them to consolidate their learning in particular areas. Or to put it another way, if you are able to answer questions from, say, history, physics and Spanish in quick succession, this will build your general confidence and, one hopes, spur you to undertake further studies.

At the same time, however, the book also seeks to stimulate and entertain. Some of the questions are drawn from areas not normally covered in secondary schools today, but which are nevertheless important to the development of a knowledgeable and well-rounded adolescent. It is hoped that such questions may prompt class discussion and lead students to undertake independent reading on matters of interest. After all, learning should not be so compartmentalised that students are discouraged from pursuing knowledge simply because it is not on the syllabus.

As to entertainment, quiz matches and trivia competitions have long been popular in Jamaica and elsewhere. Adults and students alike may match their knowledge and skills against each other in friendly rivalry, learning as they go along. This may help to reinforce the idea that education, when properly structured, can be synonymous with enjoyment.

The questions herein are developed by the author based on information drawn from a wide range of sources. While they reflect the general level of questions posed in School's Challenge Quiz presented by TVJ — and are similar to those questions — they are not taken directly from that competition, and TVJ has neither sponsored nor supported this publication.

Stephen Vasciannie
January 2003

Contents

Quiz No. 1 1

Quiz No. 2 11

Quiz No. 3 21

Quiz No. 4 31

Quiz No. 5 41

Quiz No. 6 51

Quiz No. 7 61

Quiz No. 8 71

Quiz No. 9 81

Quiz No. 10 91

Quiz No. 11 101

Quiz No. 12 111

Quiz No. 13 121

Quiz No. 14 131

Quiz No. 15 141

Quiz No. 16 151

Bibliography 161

Quiz No. 1

I. Alternate Section

Chemistry

1. What is the electronic configuration of magnesium?
   Ans. 2, 8, 2

2. What is the electronic configuration of argon?
   Ans. 2, 8, 8

Biology

3. True or false? A typical plant cell has a cellulose cell wall while a typical animal cell has no cell wall.
   Ans. True

4. True or false? A typical plant cell has a cell membrane while a typical animal cell has no cell membrane.
   Ans. False

Literature

5. Which Cuban poet wrote the poem *Sensemaya: A Chant for Killing A Snake*?
   Ans. Nicholas Guillen

6. Which Barbadian wrote the poem *The Emigrants*, and a book with the same title?
   Ans. Edward Brathwaite

Physics

7. What term denotes the reflection of a sound wave back to its source in sufficient strength and with sufficient time lag to be separately distinguished by the human ear?
   Ans. Echo

8. What term denotes an atmospheric optical illusion in which an observer sees a non-existent body of water or an image of some other object?
   Ans. Mirage

Mathematics

9. What is the value of $3^3 - 3$?
   Ans. 24

10. What is the value of $4^3 - 4$?
    Ans. 60

11. Which book of the Bible tells the story of the conversion of Saul?
    Ans. Acts of the Apostles

12. Which book of the Bible tells the story of Joseph becoming the governor of Egypt?
    Ans. Genesis

Foreign Languages

13. What is the meaning of the Spanish expression: *un dia de primavera*?
    Ans.. A spring day

14. What is the meaning of the Spanish expression: *una tarde de verano*?
    Ans. A summer afternoon (or evening)

History

15. What was the name of the central office in Seville which maintained and administered Spain's commercial monopoly over its colonies in the New World, in the 16th century?
    Ans. The Casa de Contratacion (House of Trade)

16. Name the Dominican friar who condemned Arawak slavery and servitude before an audience of influential settlers in Santo Domingo during his Whitsuntide sermon of 1511.
    Ans. Montesinos

General Knowledge

17. Who sculpted the statue of Jamaican National Hero Paul Bogle, which stands outside the Morant Bay Courthouse?
    Ans. Edna Manley

18. Who sculpted the statues of Jamaican National Heroes Sir Alexander Bustamante and Norman Manley, which stand in the centre of Kingston?
    Ans. Alvin Marriot

Geography

19. What term in geography denotes a low mound of sand and gravel which projects from the land into the sea? It is built up by waves and currents from material worn away from another part of the coast.
    Ans. Spit

20. What term in geography denotes a deposit of magma which is forced between layers of sedimentary rocks under the ground? When the magma hardens it forms a nearly horizontal sheet of igneous rock.
    Ans. Sill

Literature

21. In which Shakespearean play does Antonio borrow money from Shylock?
    Ans. *The Merchant of Venice*

22. In which Shakespearean play does Mark Antony make a famous address to friends, Romans and countrymen, following a political assassination?
    Ans. *Julius Caesar*

General Knowledge

23. With which Caribbean country do you associate the leaders Forbes Burnham and Cheddi Jagan?
    Ans. Guyana

24. With which Caribbean country do you associate the leaders Errol Barrow and Tom Adams?
    Ans. Barbados

Physics

25. What is the kinetic energy possessed by a body of mass 10 kilograms moving at a velocity of 2 m/s?
    Ans. 20 Joules

26. What is the kinetic energy possessed by a body of mass 8 kilograms moving at a velocity of 4 m/s?
    Ans. 64 Joules

History

27. In what year did the French Revolution begin?
    Ans. 1789

28. In what year did the American Civil War begin?

Ans. 1861

Chemistry

29. Arrange the following in order of decreasing activity: potassium, iron, zinc.

Ans. Potassium, zinc, iron

30. Arrange the following in order of decreasing activity: magnesium, calcium, silver.

Ans. Calcium, magnesium, silver

Local and International Affairs

31. In Barbados, which political party's name is abbreviated as the BLP?

Ans. The Barbados Labour Party

32. In Guyana, which political party's name is abbreviated as the PPP?

Ans. The People's Political Party

Mathematics

33. What is the value of 16^2 divided by 4^2?

Ans. 16

34. What is the value of 27^2 divided by 3^2?

Ans. 81

Sports

35. In which European country were the World Cup Football finals held in 1990?

Ans. Italy

36. Which European country won the World Cup Football competition in 1990?

Ans. West Germany

Theatre and Cinema

37. Name the actor who starred in the *Die Hard* series of movies.

Ans. Bruce Willis

38. Name the actor who starred in the *Dirty Harry* series of movies.

Ans. Clint Eastwood

Biology

39. True or false? When you straighten your arm, both the biceps and triceps relax.

Ans. False

40. True or false? When you straighten your arm, the biceps contract and the triceps relax?

Ans. False

II. The Speed Section

Speed Questions for Team A

1. What is the value of Sin 0?
   Ans. 0

2. In which Caribbean country would you find the town of St. George's?
   Ans. Grenada

3. What is the French for "the city".
   Ans. *La cite*

4. As we go across Period 3 of the Periodic Table from left to right, is there an increase or decrease in atomic size?
   Ans. Decrease

5. Which Jamaican wrote the poem entitled *Noh Lickle Twang!*?
   Ans. Louise Bennett

6. Which is longer: the Old or the New Testament?
   Ans. The Old Testament

7. Give the name of the newspaper edited by Edward Jordan in Jamaica in the early 1830s.
   Ans. *The Watchman and Jamaica Free Press* (or *The Watchman*)

8. Which is the "flight and fright" hormone?
   Ans. Adrenaline

9. In which continent will the World Cup Football Competition be held in the year 2006?
   Ans. Africa

10. Identify the longest canal in the world.
    Ans. The Grand Canal of China

11. Complete the Jamaican proverb: "Long road draw sweat ..."
    Ans. "... short cut draw blood."

12. Which Jamaican parish capital's name means "plain by the sea"?
    Ans. Savanna-la-Mar

13. Who wrote the novel *David Copperfield*?
    Ans. Charles Dickens

14. What precipitate is formed when lead nitrate reacts with sodium chloride?
    Ans. Lead (II) chloride

15. During pregnancy, what links the placenta of the mother to the abdomen of the foetus?
    Ans. The umbilical cord

16. What is the value in the decimal system of 111 to the base 2?
    Ans. 7

17. During the apprenticeship period in the British West Indies, by what other name were the Special Magistrates known?
    Ans. Stipendiary Magistrates

18. Give the English for the French *les vetements*.
    Ans. Clothes

19. Which actor starred in the movie *High Noon*?
    Ans. Gary Cooper

20. A vehicle covers a distance of 31 kilometres in 2 hours. What is its speed in kilometres per hour, expressed as a mixed number?

   Ans. $15\frac{1}{2}$ km/hr

21. Is the island of St. Vincent north or south of the equator?

   Ans. North

22. Spell the word VOCABULARY.

23. What name did the Arawaks give to their priests?

   Ans. Boyos

24. With which sport do you associate the names Tiger Woods and Gary Player?

   Ans. Golf

25. In which river did John the Baptist baptize Jesus?

   Ans. The Jordan River

26. What is the past participle of the verb "sing"?

   Ans. Sung

27. In which Jamaican parish is the town of Mocho located?

   Ans. Clarendon

28. State the formula for the chloride ion?

   Ans. Cl^-

29. What is the meaning of the Spanish *la iglesia*?

   Ans. The church

30. If you were a chiropodist, what part of the body would be your main area of concern?

   Ans. Feet

31. Which of the following parts of the eye is transparent: the sclera or the cornea?

   Ans. The cornea

32. Who founded the Society of Jesus, or the Jesuits?

   Ans. St. Ignatius of Loyola

33. Who preceded Tony Blair as the Prime Minister of Great Britain?

   Ans. John Major

34. In which country would you find the headquarters of CARICOM: Barbados, Guyana or St. Lucia?

   Ans. Guyana

35. How many centimetres are there in 4.5 metres?

   Ans. 450

36. What kind of combination, covalent or electrovalent, is expected to take place between sodium and sulphur?

   Ans. Electrovalent

37. Give the meaning of the Spanish word *aunque*.

   Ans. Although

38. In what country was the Latin American revolutionary Che Guevara born?

   Ans. Argentina

39. According to the proverb, who calls the tune?

   Ans. He who pays the piper.

40. State the chemical formula for sodium hydrogen carbonate.

   Ans. $NaHCO_3$

Speed Questions for Team B

1. What is the value of Sin 30?
   Ans. $\frac{1}{2}$

2. In which Caribbean country would you find the town of Plymouth?
   Ans. Montserrat

3. What is the French for "science".
   Ans. *La science*

4. As we go across Period 3 of the Periodic Table from left to right, there is a change from non-metals to metals. True or false?
   Ans. False

5. Which Jamaican wrote the poems *Litany* and *History Makers*?
   Ans. George Campbell

6. Which is longer: the book of Psalms or the book of Revelations?
   Ans. Psalms

7. In what year did the "Jamaica Rebellion" in the western parishes of the island take place?
   Ans. 1831

8. Thyroxin, insulin, pepsin. A deficiency of which of these is likely to cause obesity and sluggishness?
   Ans. Thyroxin

9. In which continent was the first World Cup Football Competition held?
   Ans. South America

10. Identify the largest lake in the world.
    Ans. The Caspian Sea

11. Complete the Jamaican proverb: "Old fire stick ..."
    Ans. "... ketch easy."

12. Which Jamaican parish capital did Christopher Columbus call Santa Gloria?
    Ans. St. Ann's Bay

13. Who wrote the novel *The Adventures of Huckleberry Finn*?
    Ans. Mark Twain

14. What precipitate is formed when barium chloride reacts with sodium sulphate?
    Ans. Barium sulphate

15. What term in biology denotes the microscopic cell organelles that act as the powerhouses of the cell?
    Ans. Mitochondria

16. What is the equivalent in the decimal system of 100 to the base 2?
    Ans. 4

17. Which was the first free village established in Jamaica, following the abolition of slavery?
    Ans. Sligoville

18. Give the English for the French *le voleur*.
    Ans. The thief

19. Which actress starred in the movie *The Silence of the Lambs*?
    Ans. Jodie Foster

20. A vehicle, travelling with a speed of 12 kilometres per hour, moves for $2\frac{1}{4}$ hours. How far has it travelled?
    Ans. 27 kilometres

21. Which lie further north on the map: the Leeward or the Windward Islands?
    Ans. The Leeward Islands

22. Spell the word CREATIVITY.

23. What name did the Arawaks give to their hammocks?
    Ans. Hamaca

24. With which sport do you associate the names Pete Sampras and Rod Laver?
    Ans. Tennis

25. Name one of the two disciples whom Jesus promised to make into "fishers of men".
    Ans. Simon (Peter); Andrew

26. What is the past participle of the verb "educate"?
    Ans. Educated

27. In which Jamaican parish is the town of Little London located?
    Ans. Westmoreland

28. State the formula for the sodium ion.
    Ans. Na^+

29. What is the meaning of the Spanish *el hombre*?
    Ans. The man

30. If you were a dermatologist, what part of the body would be your main area of concern?
    Ans. The skin

31. Which part of the eye is a muscular diaphragm that regulates the size of the pupil: the iris or the choroid?
    Ans. The iris

32. Who prompted the start of the Protestant Reformation with his "95 theses"?
    Ans. Martin Luther

33. Who preceded Bill Clinton as the President of the United States of America?
    Ans. George Bush

34. In which country would you find the headquarters of the Caribbean Development Bank: Guyana, Barbados or Belize?
    Ans. Barbados

35. How many centimetres are there in 11.75 metres?
    Ans. 1175

36. What kind of combination, covalent or electrovalent, is expected to take place between carbon and oxygen?
    Ans. Covalent

37. Give the meaning of the Spanish word *audaz*.
    Ans. Bold

38. In what country did the Latin American revolutionary Che Guevara die?
    Ans. Bolivia

39. According to the proverb, who laughs best?
    Ans. He who laughs last.

40. State the chemical formula for sodium sulphate.
    Ans. Na_2SO_4

III. The Signal Section

Music

1. Identify the early Jamaican pop group which sang the hit *Poor Me Israelite*?
    Ans. Desmond Dekker and the Aces

Theatre and Cinema

2. Which actor played the first James Bond in the movie *Dr. No*: Timothy Dalton, George Lazenby or Sean Connery?
    Ans. Sean Connery

Bible Knowledge

3. Name the Old Testament character, a God-fearing and good man from Uz, whose faith was tested by God, but who remained steadfast. He is best known as a man of patience.
    Ans. Job

Physics

4. A body of mass 50 kilograms is standing on a weighing machine. What is the reading on the weighing machine in Newtons, assuming that acceleration due to gravity is 10 metres per second squared?
    Ans. 500 Newtons

Foreign Languages

5. Give the meaning of the Spanish saying: *La practica hace al maestro*?
    Ans. Practice makes perfect.

Local and International Affairs

6. What international position has each of the following held in common: Boutros Boutros Ghali, Kurt Waldheim, Kofi Annan and U Thant?
    Ans. Post of Secretary-General of the United Nations

Mathematics

7. State the value of $\frac{3}{5}$ in standard form.
    Ans. 6×10^{-1}

Music

8. Which female voice is between contralto and soprano?
    Ans. Mezzo-soprano

Biology

9. What term denotes the delivery of a baby through surgical incision in the wall of the abdomen and womb?
    Ans. Caesarean Section

Literature

10. Name the author of the book *A House for Mr. Biswas*.
    Ans. V.S. Naipaul

Chemistry

11. What term in chemistry denotes the process in which current is passed through an electrolyte?
    Ans. Electrolysis

Foreign Languages

12. Give the meaning of the French term: *Il fait froid*.
    Ans. It is cold.

General Knowledge

13. What is the meaning of the abbreviation G.D.P. in economics?
    Ans. Gross Domestic Product

Music

14. Which Jamaican entertainer, Beenie Man, Ninjaman or Cocoa Tea, was given the name Desmond Ballantine at birth?

    Ans. Ninjaman

Jamaican Heritage

15. Which Jamaican National Hero described Governor Eyre in the following terms: "I have never seen an animal more voracious for cruelty and power than the present Governor of Jamaica."?

    Ans. George William Gordon

Theatre and Cinema

16. Name the actor who played the lead role of Ivan in the Jamaican movie *The Harder They Come*?

    Ans. Jimmy Cliff

Bible Knowledge

17. Which king threw Shadrach, Meshach and Abednego into a fiery furnace for refusing to bow down and worship an idol?

    Ans. Nebuchadnezzar

Physics

18. When a wire moves in a magnetic field, the electric current induced in the wire generates a magnetic field that tends to oppose the movement. This is a statement of whose law in physics?

    Ans. Lenz's Law

Biology

19. What type of joint is formed where the femur meets the pelvis: is it ball and socket, hinged or fixed?

    Ans. Ball and socket

English Language

20. Give the meaning of the figurative expression "to hit below the belt".

    Ans. To act unfairly in a contest

Local and International Affairs

21. What is the meaning of the abbreviation WHO in international affairs?

    Ans. World Health Organization

Sports

22. Which famous Australian cricketer had a test average of 99.94 in Test cricket: Richie Benaud, Ian Chappell or Don Bradman?

    Ans. Don Bradman

Literature

23. Which West Indian wrote the novel *The Sure Salvation*?

    Ans. John Hearne

Art

24. Name the Italian artist who is responsible for the most famous painting of *The Last Supper*.

    Ans. Leonardo Da Vinci

Geography

25. This country has cities which include Cork and Limerick, and its capital is at Dublin. Name the country.

    Ans. Ireland

Mathematics

26. If $\frac{24}{x^2} = \frac{1}{6}$, what is the positive value of x?

    Ans. 12

History

27. In what century did the first British and French settlements in St. Kitts begin: the 15th, 16th or 17th century?
    Ans. The 17th century

Foreign Languages

28. Give the meaning of the Spanish *la cena*.
    Ans. Supper

General Knowledge

29. In an alphabetical listing of the books of the Bible, which would appear last?
    Ans. Zephaniah

Physics

30. Which form of electromagnetic radiation has wavelengths just shorter than those of visible light: ultraviolet, microwave or infra-red rays?
    Ans. Ultraviolet rays

Bible Knowledge

31. Name the Babylonian king who destroyed the Temple at Jerusalem and brought the Jewish people to Babylon and into captivity.
    Ans. Nebuchadnezzar

Chemistry

32. Sn is the chemical symbol for which element?
    Ans. Tin

English Language

33. Give one word for the stick used by a musical conductor, or by a policeman.
    Ans. Baton

Geography

34. In which Caribbean State would you find the Demarara, Essequibo and Berbice Rivers, as well as a bauxite mining town named Linden?
    Ans. Guyana

Literature

35. Which Shakespearean play, featuring three prophetic witches, includes the prediction that Birnamwood would go to Dunsinane?
    Ans. *Macbeth*

Mathematics

36. If $x^2 - 9 = 0$, what are the two values of x?
    Ans. 3, ⁻3

General Knowledge

37. Identify the American city, located in the state of Illinois, which is often referred to as the "Windy City".
    Ans. Chicago

History

38. In what year was the University of the West Indies founded: 1938, 1948 or 1958?
    Ans. 1948

Mythology

39. Which god in Roman mythology was identified with the Greek god Hermes?
    Ans. Mercury

Bible Knowledge

40. True or false? Methuselah was Noah's grandfather.
    Ans. True

Quiz No. 2

I. Alternate Section

Local and International Affairs

1. The pronunciation of the name of which African country was changed on independence to highlight the name of the country's president?
   Ans. Kenya

2. Which Mediterranean island is partitioned with the northern 40 per cent being under Turkish control?
   Ans. Cyprus

Physics

3. True or false? Lasting interference patterns can appear if waves have roughly the same amplitude.
   Ans. True

4. True or false? Lasting interference patterns can appear if waves are roughly the same type.
   Ans. False

History

5. What name did the Arawaks give to the chief of each village?
   Ans. Cacique

6. At the time of Columbus' arrival in the West Indies, the Arawaks acknowledged the greater authority of a cacique living on which island?
   Ans. Cuba

English Language

7. Give the meaning of the figurative expression "Draconian legislation".
   Ans. Very severe laws

8. Explain the figurative expression "back in harness".
   Ans. To resume work after a holiday

Biology

9. A deficiency of which vitamin is likely to give rise to beri beri?
   Ans. Vitamin B1 (Thiamine)

10. A deficiency of which vitamin is likely to give rise to scurvy?
    Ans. Vitamin C

General Knowledge

11. In which city in Trinidad would you find a statue of Mahatma Gandhi?
    Ans. San Fernando

12. In which Caribbean city would you find a controversial roundabout named in honour of Dame Nita Barrow?
    Ans. Bridgetown

Chemistry

13. What is the atomic number of bromine?
    Ans. 35

14. What is the atomic number of calcium?
    Ans. 20

Sports

15. In which Caribbean territory would you find the Mindoo Phillip Park, sometimes used for first-class cricket: St. Lucia, Grenada or Barbados?
    Ans. St. Lucia

16. Name the main Test cricket ground in Guyana.
    Ans. Bourda

Music

17. In music, what is meant by the term *sotto voce*?
    Ans. A passage performed in an undertone

18. In music, what is meant by the term syncopation?
    Ans. Shifting of the accent on to a beat not normally accented

Mathematics

19. Evaluate 5% of 400 plus 20% of 20.
    Ans. 24

20. Evaluate $12\frac{1}{2}$% of 96 plus 10% of 10.
    Ans. 13

Geography

21. Identify the most easterly of the mountains in Jamaica.
    Ans. John Crow Mountain

22. Identify the mountain which marks the centre of Jamaica.
    Ans. Bull Head Mountain

Literature

23. Who wrote the novel *The Grapes of Wrath*?
    Ans. John Steinbeck

24. Who wrote the novel *A Passage to India*?
    Ans. E.M. Forster

Foreign Languages

25. In Spain, what is *el incendio*?
    Ans. The fire

26. Give the meaning of the Spanish term *preferido*.
    Ans. Favourite

Art

27. Name the French painter and sculptor who painted *Joy of Life*.
    Ans. Henri Matisse

28. Which artist painted *La Maja Desnuda*?
    Ans. Goya

Physics

29. In physics, what is the meaning of the term "plastic behaviour"?
    Ans. The permanent change in shape or size in some solids when stress is applied beyond a certain value (the yield point)

30. In physics, what is a hydraulic machine?
    Ans. One in which the pressure of a liquid is used to transfer energy.

Foreign Languages

31. Give the meaning of the French word *actuellement*.
    Ans. At the present time

32. Give the meaning of the French term *au-dessous de*.
    Ans. Below

Bible Knowledge

33. According to the Gospel of St. Luke, which angel announced the birth of Jesus to Mary?
    Ans. Gabriel

34. Which Old Testament character was noted both for his many wives and for his friendship with Jonathan?
    Ans. David

English Language

35. Spell the word APPARATUS.

36. Spell the word HAEMORRHAGE.

Theatre and Cinema

37. For her performance in the movie *Mary Poppins*, who won the Best Actress Oscar in 1964?
    Ans. Julie Andrews

38. For her performance in the movie *Terms of Endearment*, who won the Best Actress Oscar in 1983?
    Ans. Shirley MacLaine

History

39. In what year was the Negro Education Grant introduced for the British West Indian colonies?
    Ans. 1835

40. In what year was the Sugar Duties Act passed by the British Government?
    Ans. 1846

II. The Speed Section

Speed Questions for Team A

1. Which West Indian wrote the novel *A Flag on the Island*?
   Ans. V.S. Naipaul

2. Who was the first Prime Minister of Trinidad and Tobago?
   Ans. Eric Williams

3. Complete the Jamaican proverb: "Disobedient pickney ..."
   Ans. "... nyam rock stone."

4. Name the Russian painter traditionally regarded as the originator of abstract art.
   Ans. Vassily Kandinsky

5. Which has the longer average life span: the ostrich or the goat?
   Ans. Ostrich

6. Name the science that studies the flow of fluids.
   Ans. Hydraulics

7. Which metal has an ore known as beryl?
   Ans. Beryllium

8. Explain the figurative expression "to die in harness".
   Ans. To continue one's occupation until death

9. With which musical instrument do you associate Yehudi Menuhin?
   Ans. The violin

10. What letter is often used in physics to denote acceleration due to gravity?
    Ans. g

11. Which Italian revolutionary formed the Young Italy movement in 1831?
    Ans. Giuseppe Manzini

12. Spell the word CURIOSITY.

13. In what year did *One Flew Over the Cuckoo's Nest* capture most major oscars at the Annual Academy Awards: 1965, 1975 or 1985?
    Ans. 1975

14. What is the meaning of the acronym LIAT?
    Ans. Leeward Islands Air Transport

15. In which Jamaican parish is Blue Mountain Peak located?
    Ans. St. Thomas

16. What is the height of a pile of 30 books each $\frac{5}{4}$ cm thick?
    Ans. 18 cm

17. Which has the higher specific gravity: tin or tar?
    Ans. Tin

18. True or false? Lasting interference patterns can appear if waves have roughly the same wavelength.
    Ans. True

19. Give the plural of the word octopus.
    Ans. Octopuses or octopi

20. Which Jamaican port derives its name from the fair weather for travelling to Cuba which Columbus encountered there?
    Ans. Montego Bay

21. How many points are awarded for a touchdown in American Football?
    Ans. 6

22. Spell the word SYLLABUS.

23. What term denotes the property of a metal which allows it to be beaten into a sheet?
    Ans. Malleability

24. What name is given in golf to the specially placed surface in which the hole is situated?
    Ans. Green

25. Pronounce the Spanish for "the sign".
    Ans. *El signo*, or *la señal*

26. An article is purchased for $400 and sold for $420. What is the percentage profit?
    Ans. 5%

27. In what year was the Great Plague in London?
    Ans. 1665

28. Name the main airport in Grenada.
    Ans. Point Salines International Airport

29. Which is greater: $(\frac{1}{4})^{-2}$ or $16^{\frac{1}{2}}$?
    Ans. $(\frac{1}{4})^{-2}$

30. In which book would you find the line "All animals are equal, but some animals are more equal than others"?
    Ans. *Animal Farm*

31. True or false? In wave theory, the whole space in which there is overlap is known as a displacement region.
    Ans. False (Interference region)

32. Which university is known by the abbreviation MIT?
    Ans. Massachusetts Institute of Technology

33. Give the meaning of the figurative expression: "In Davy Jones' locker".
    Ans. At the bottom of the sea

34. For which product is the town of Middle Quarters specially known?
    Ans. Shrimps

35. What is the meaning of the French word *propre*?
    Ans. Clean, or own

36. What is the negative of the reciprocal of $-\frac{1}{5}$?
    Ans. 5

37. By what name is trinitrotoluene better known?
    Ans. TNT

38. Give the meaning of the Latin phrase *Ave Maria*.
    Ans. Hail Mary

39. Which Russian author wrote *The Brothers Karamazov*?
    Ans. Fyodor Dostoyevsky

40. What is a sarcophagus?
    Ans. A stone coffin, especially one made of limestone.

1. Which West Indian wrote the novel
   Fireflies?
   Ans. Shiva Naipaul

2. Who was the first, and only, Prime
   Minister of the West Indies Federation?
   Ans. Grantley Adams

3. Complete the Jamaican proverb: "Big
   blanket ..."
   Ans. "... mek man sleep late."

4. Name the French sculptor responsible
   for *The Thinker*.
   Ans. Auguste Rodin

5. Which has the longer average life span:
   the dog or the goose?
   Ans. Goose

6. Name the branch of chemistry which
   deals with all compounds other than
   those of carbon.
   Ans. Inorganic chemistry

7. Which metal has an ore known as
   smaltite?
   Ans. Cobalt

8. Which figurative expression reminds us
   that good fortune is usually the
   forerunner of great prosperity?
   Ans. It never rains but it pours.

9. Who composed the ballet *Romeo and
   Juliet*?
   Ans. Sergei Prokofiev

10. What letter is often used in physics to
    denote the speed of light?
    Ans. c

11. What name was given to the 1820
    conspiracy in England to assassinate
    cabinet ministers?
    Ans. The Cato Street Conspiracy

12. Spell the word BAZAAR.

13. In what year did *Kramer vs. Kramer*
    capture several major oscars at the
    Annual Academy Awards: 1969, 1979
    or 1989?
    Ans. 1979

14. What is the meaning of the abbreviation
    BWIA?
    Ans. British West Indian Airways

15. In which Jamaican parish is the Sugar
    Loaf Peak located?
    Ans. Portland

16. What is the height of a pile of 25 books
    each $\frac{4}{5}$ cm thick?
    Ans. 20 cm

17. Which has the higher specific gravity:
    silver or steel?
    Ans. Silver

18. True or false? Lasting interference
    patterns can appear if waves pass
    through the same space at the same
    time.
    Ans. True

19. Give the plural of the word referendum.
    Ans. Referenda

20. Who was the first mistress of the Rose
    Hall Estate in Jamaica?
    Ans. Rosa Palmer

21. How many points are awarded for a goal in Australian Rules Football?

    Ans. 6

22. Spell the word TYPHOID.

23. Give one word for a substance that does not conduct electricity.

    Ans. Insulator; non-conductor

24. What name is given in golf to the starting place for a hole or peg on which the ball is placed?

    Ans. Tee

25. Pronounce the Spanish for "the saint".

    Ans. *El santo*

26. An article is purchased for $250 and sold for $275. What is the percentage profit?

    Ans. 10%

27. In what year was the Great Fire of London?

    Ans. 1666

28. Name the main airport in Trinidad and Tobago.

    Ans. Piarco

29. Which is greater: 3^{-3} or $(\frac{1}{3})^2$?

    Ans. $(\frac{1}{3})^2$

30. What name was George Orwell given at birth?

    Ans. Eric Blair

31. True or false? In wave theory, two or more waves of the same type cannot exist in the same place at the same time without interference.

    Ans. True

32. Which university is known by the abbreviation LSE?

    Ans. London School of Economics

33. Give the meaning of the figurative expression: "Devil's bones".

    Ans. Dice

34. In which Jamaican parish is the town of Middle Quarters located?

    Ans. St. Elizabeth

35. What, in French, is *le sac a main*?

    Ans. Handbag

36. How many times can 0.05 be taken from 5?

    Ans. 100 times

37. By what name is acetylsalicylic acid better known?

    Ans. Aspirin

38. Give the meaning of the Latin phrase *id est*.

    Ans. That is

39. Which Russian author wrote *The Cherry Orchard*?

    Ans. Anton Chekhov

40. What is euthanasia?

    Ans. Mercy killing

III. The Signal Section

Physics

1. What voltage will drive a current of 4 amperes through a resistance of 20 ohms?
   Ans. 80 volts

Mathematics

2. What is the value of $\frac{3}{10}$ plus $\frac{7}{100}$, stated as a decimal?
   Ans. 0.37

Art

3. Which French post-impressionist painter abandoned his society to live and paint in Tahiti?
   Ans. Paul Gauguin

General Knowledge

4. An 18th century historian once called Orange Cove "beautiful beyond description". In which Jamaican parish is it located: Hanover, Westmoreland or St. Ann?
   Ans. Hanover

Sports

5. Name the cricketer from Swetes, Antigua, whose mother used to ring a bell whenever he took a wicket in Test cricket.
   Ans. Courtley Ambrose

Biology

6. True or false? Ectothermic animals are warm-blooded.
   Ans. False

English Language

7. Which idiomatic expression denotes a victory which is as costly as defeat?
   Ans. A Pyrrhic victory

History

8. Which Egyptian made the first recorded observations of angles of incidence and refraction?
   Ans. Ptolemy

Music

9. With which musical instrument do you associate the Jamaican Ernie Ranglin?
   Ans. The guitar

Chemistry

10. Which element has the lowest boiling point: hydrogen, helium or oxygen?
    Ans. Helium

Proverbs and Idioms

11. Give the meaning of the Jamaican proverb "Y'eye lash owla dan byade".
    Ans. We must acknowledge with respect those older and wiser than ourselves.

Geography

12. In which parish of Jamaica would you find the Rio Grande and the Swift River?
    Ans. Portland

Mathematics

13. If $\sin^2 x = 0.35$, what is the value of $\cos^2 x$?
    Ans. 0.65

Art

14. Identify the Greek sculptor and architect who constructed the Parthenon.
    Ans. Phidias

Physics

15. At constant temperature, the volume of a gas is inversely proportional to the pressure exerted on it. This is a statement of which of the gas laws?
    Ans. Boyle's Law

Religious Knowledge

16. Which of Jesus' disciples healed the lame man at Gate Beautiful?
    Ans. Peter

Chemistry

17. What is the functional group of an alcohol: is it OH, O or CHO?
    Ans. OH

Literature

18. Who wrote the novel *The Mayor of Casterbridge*?
    Ans. Thomas Hardy

Mythology

19. Which mythological character was condemned by the Olympians to stand at the western edge of the earth, supporting the heavens on his head and his shoulders?
    Ans. Atlas

General Knowledge

20. Name the largest of the nine planets which orbit the sun.
    Ans. Jupiter

Foreign Languages

21. Which French term denotes both "the waiter" and "the boy"?
    Ans. *Le garcon*

Sports

22. Whom did the then Cassius Clay defeat in 1964 to win the world heavyweight title for the first time?
    Ans. Sonny Liston

History

23. In what year was the People's National Party founded in Jamaica?
    Ans. 1938

Biology

24. Is bulimia an eating disorder, a species of fish or a type of dance?
    Ans. An eating disorder

Local and International Affairs

25. Who preceded Kofi Annan as the Secretary General of the United Nations?
    Ans. Boutros-Boutros Ghali

English Language

26. Form a noun from the adjective "rich".
    Ans. Richness; riches

Music

27. Which composer, the most popular of all Russian composers with Western audiences, has works which include the *1812 Overture* and the ballet *Swan Lake*?
    Ans. Tchaikovsky

Religious Knowledge

28. By what other name is the Church of St. Thomas the Apostle, located at South Parade in Kingston, better known?
    Ans. The Kingston Parish Church

Mathematics

29. How many full packages, each weighing 26 grams can be made from a larger package weighing 780 grams?
    Ans. 30

History

30. Who married Eva Braun on April 29, 1945, on the day before he committed suicide with her in an underground shelter?
    Ans. Adolf Hitler

Bible Knowledge

31. What were the names of Jacob's two wives?
    Ans. Leah and Rachel

Biology

32. Which part of the body is affected by myopia?
    Ans. The eye

Sports

33. Born 1940, this footballer scored over 1200 goals for Santos and Brazil, and starred in the 1958 and 1970 World Cup competitions. His full name is Edson Arantes do Nascimento. Give his popular name.
    Ans. Pelé

Physics

34. State the first law of refraction.
    Ans. The incident and refracted rays are on opposite sides of and in the same plane as the normal.

Geography

35. Which geographical term, denoting a flat-topped upland, is derived from the Spanish for "table"?
    Ans. Mesa

Literature

36. Identify the Shakespearean play which begins with the words: "If music be the food of love, play on, Give me excess of it ..."
    Ans. *Twelfth Night*

Chemistry

37. Which metal has an ore known as siderite: lead, iron or tin?
    Ans. Iron

Music

38. By what name is the calypsonian Slinger Fransisco more generally known?
    Ans. The Mighty Sparrow

General Knowledge

39. What national honour is held by Lady Bustamante in Jamaica: Order of the Nation, Order of Distinction or Order of Jamaica?
    Ans. Order of Jamaica

Mathematics

40. What is the value of Cos 0 degrees multiplied by 5?
    Ans. 5

Quiz No. 3

I. Alternate Section

Literature

1. This novel by a West Indian features Rocha, a South African revolutionary in exile. Name it.
   Ans. *Guerillas* (by V.S. Naipaul)

2. Give the full title of the book by V.S. Naipaul which begins as follows: "Sometimes old India, the old, eternal India many Indians like to talk about, does seem just to go on".
   Ans. *India: A Wounded Civilization*

General Knowledge

3. Identify the Caribbean head of government who once made a speech under the title "History will absolve me".
   Ans. Fidel Castro

4. Whose dying words were: "So little done, so much to do"?
   Ans. Cecil Rhodes

Mathematics

5. What is the sum of the whole numbers from 1 to 40?
   Ans. 820

6. What is the 11th term of the series: 7, 16, 25...?
   Ans. 97

History

7. By which treaty was the War of Jenkins Ear brought to an end in 1748?
   Ans. Aix-la-Chapelle

8. Which battle of 1954 marked the end of French influence in Indochina?
   Ans. Dien Bien Phu

Jamaican Heritage

9. Which part of Kingston, first called "Smith Village", had its name changed in honour of a Governor of Jamaica from the 1930s?
   Ans. Denham Town

10. Who was the Governor of Jamaica in 1738 when the British made peace with the Maroons?
    Ans. Edward Trelawny

Geography

11. What name is given to lines on a map joining places of equal magnetic declination?
    Ans. Isogonic lines

12. In geography, what are kames?
    Ans. Mounds of sand and gravel deposited by streams which flow from the snouts of glaciers.

Foreign Languages

13. What is the meaning of the Spanish command *Traigamelo*?
    Ans. Bring it to me.

14. What is the meaning of the Spanish command *Vistase*?
    Ans. Get dressed.

Music

15. Which artiste, who rose to popularity in the 1980s, did the song entitled *Give me a Reason*?
    Ans. Tracy Chapman

16. *Who Let the Dogs Out* was a popular hit from the 1990s most associated with which group of singers?
    Ans. Baha Men

Chemistry

17. In compounds containing hydrogen, the hydrogen atom has an oxidation number of +1, except in hydrides such as MgH_2, in which hydrogen has an oxidation number of what?
    Ans. ⁻1

18. In chemistry, which method is usually adopted for finding the molecular weight of a gaseous hydrogen: Victor Meyer's Method, the Eudiometer Method, or Hoffmann's Method?
    Ans. Eudiometer Method

Literature

19. In the novel *Moll Flanders*, Defoe depicts a woman who finally ends up as a mistress on a plantation in which U.S. State?
    Ans. Virginia

20. In Shakespeare, what superstitious man orders his wife to stand in the path of his friend so his touch can break the spell of her sterility?
    Ans. Julius Caesar

General Knowledge

21. What name given to the legislative body of some countries is derived from a Latin word meaning "old men"?
    Ans. Senate

22. What term denotes injury to the skin and sometimes tissues by freezing temperatures?
    Ans. Frostbite

Theatre and Cinema

23. In 1970, Glenda Jackson gained the Oscar for her role in the film version of a D.H. Lawrence novel. What was the name of the film?
    Ans. *Women in Love*

24. For her performance in which film did Gwyneth Paltrow win the Academy Award for Best Actress?
    Ans. *Shakespeare in Love*

Physics

25. Give another name for newton per metre squared?
    Ans. Pascal

26. What is the SI unit for the coefficient of viscosity?
    Ans. Poise, decapoise, or newton second per metre squared

History

27. Which two old Dutch colonies were united in 1831 to form British Guiana?
    Ans. Demerara and Berbice

28. Name the two countries bound by the Treaty of Tordesillas.
    Ans. Spain and Portugal

Biology

29. What is the resulting colour when Benedict's solution reacts positively for simple sugars: brick red, yellow or dark blue?

    Ans. Brick red

30. In which of the following places would you expect the nerve endings sensitive to touch to be the farthest apart: the back of the hand, the palm of the hand or the upper arm?

    Ans. The upper arm

Art

31. Which Italian artist has a famous drawing meant to depict the proportions of the human body: DaVinci, Michelangelo or Raphael

    Ans. Da Vinci

32. Whom did James Whister sue in 1878 for describing his painting, *Nocturne in Black and Gold* as "flinging a pot of paint in the public's face"?

    Ans. Ruskin

Bible Knowledge

33. In the Bible, what stood in the most holy place in the Jewish Temple?

    Ans. The Ark of the Covenant

34. What name did Abraham give to the place where he went to sacrifice Isaac?

    Ans. Jehovah Jireh

Sports

35. Who invented basketball?

    Ans. James Naismith

36. In which conference of the NBA do the Portland Trailblazers compete?

    Ans. Western Conference

Mathematics

37. Find the smallest number that must be added to 8 and 10 to make the L.C.M. 60.

    Ans. 2

38. State the value of 111_3 as a denary number.

    Ans. 13

Foreign Languages

39. What is the meaning of the French verb *jurer*?

    Ans. To swear

40. What is the meaning of the French verb *tuer*?

    Ans. To kill

II. The Speed Section

Speed Questions for Team A

1. Which West Indian wrote the novel *Tumatumari*?
   Ans. Wilson Harris

2. What does the Spanish phrase *por lo menos* mean?
   Ans. At least

3. Which biblical character said: "How are the mighty fallen"?
   Ans. David

4. In the equation $s = ut + \frac{1}{2}at^2$, what does the letter u represent?
   Ans. Initial velocity

5. Who or what is a croupier?
   Ans. One who pays out money and collects bets at a gaming table.

6. What reagent confirms the presence of lead ions in the laboratory: copper iodide, lead iodide or potassium iodide?
   Ans. Potassium iodide

7. In Jamaica, what does the term "fenke" mean?
   Ans. Weak

8. What is the fluid part of blood called?
   Ans. Plasma

9. What did Elisha Otis invent?
   Ans. The passenger elevator

10. What is the square root of 0.0009?
    Ans. 0.03

11. In what year did the Titanic sink?
    Ans. 1912

12. What is the meaning of the acronym JUPOPE?
    Ans. Jamaica Union of Public Officers and Public Employees

13. Who composed the opera *Manon Lescaut*?
    Ans. Puccini

14. Who wrote the novel *To Kill a Mockingbird*?
    Ans. Harper Lee

15. In which parish of Jamaica would you find Halse Hall?
    Ans. Clarendon

16. Which European artist did an equestrian portrait of Charles I?
    Ans. Van Dyke

17. Who is described as a man of straw?
    Ans. An insubstantial person

18. In which country was the writer Jamaica Kincaid born?
    Ans. Antigua

19. State the nationality of the former tennis player Mary Pierce?
    Ans. French

20. Name the male star of the 1990s movie *Bait*.
    Ans. Jamie Foxx

21. How do you say the North Sea in French?
    Ans. *La mer du Nord*

22. What is the value of Sin 150 degrees?
    Ans. $\frac{1}{2}$

23. Which of the following waves does not travel at the speed of light: microwaves, x-rays, or ultrasonic waves?
    Ans. Ultrasonic

24. Chlorophyll is soluble in which of the following: water, benzene or alcohol?
    Ans. Alcohol

25. What is the Spanish for magazine?
    Ans. *La revista*

26. What is the usual shape of a shield volcano?
    Ans. Like that of an upturned saucer

27. In what century was the Gothic architectural style introduced?
    Ans. 12th century

28. Who won the Norman Manley Award for Excellence in 1983 for his contribution to religion?
    Ans. Hugh Sherlock

29. Which element has the symbol Kr?
    Ans. Krypton

30. In the history of Test cricket, which batsman has the third highest score for a single innings?
    Ans. Len Hutton

31. What is the meaning of the musical term "fine"?
    Ans. The end

32. How long did the Plague of Darkness remain in the land of Egypt?
    Ans. 3 days

33. Spell the word COALESCE.

34. Which French Revolutionary leader spearheaded the Reign of Terror?
    Ans. Robespierre

35. What is the French for "to lose weight"?
    Ans. *Maigrir*

36. State the official language of Ethiopia.
    Ans. Amharic

37. Who was known as the father of modern painting?
    Ans. Giovanni Cimabue

38. What was the first miracle performed by Jesus?
    Ans. Turning water into wine

39. Who was the first Prime Minister of Great Britain?
    Ans. Robert Walpole

40. Who wrote *Little Lord Fauntleroy*?
    Ans. Frances Hodgson Burnett

Speed Questions for Team B

1. Which West Indian wrote the novel *A Quality of Violence*?
   Ans. Andrew Salkey

2. What is the meaning of the Spanish word *antiguo*?
   Ans. Former, ancient

3. Which of the gospels is not a synoptic gospel?
   Ans. John

4. In the equation e=mc², what is denoted by the letter "c"?
   Ans. The speed of light

5. What is xenophobia?
   Ans. Fear of strangers

6. Which well known gas was formerly known as Azote: hydrogen, oxygen or nitrogen?
   Ans. Nitrogen

7. In Jamaica, what does "kin puppalik" mean?
   Ans. To somersault

8. What is the name of the layer of fat that envelopes the nerve fibre?
   Ans. Myelin sheath

9. What is the fourth root of 625?
   Ans. 5

10. Which river is known as the "mother of Rivers"?
    Ans. The Danube

11. In what year did Columbus set out on his fourth voyage?
    Ans. 1502

12. In Jamaica, what is meant by the acronym ODPEM?
    Ans. Office of Disaster Preparedness and Emergency Management

13. Who composed the opera *Cosi Fan Tuti*?
    Ans. Mozart

14. Who wrote the novel *The Call of the Wild*?
    Ans. Jack London

15. In which parish of Jamaica would you find the town of Rio Bueno?
    Ans. Trelawny

16. Who painted *The Fighting Temeraire*?
    Ans. JMW Turner

17. In which country was the poet Derek Walcott born?
    Ans. St. Lucia

18. What is meant by the word "fuselage"?
    Ans. The body of an aeroplane

19. Jason Gillespie was a national sporting representative in which sport?
    Ans. Cricket

21. How do you say Prime Minister in French?
    Ans. *Le Premier Ministre*

22. Two dice are thrown together. What is the probability that the sum will be seven?
    Ans. $\frac{1}{6}$

23. True or false? The mass of gas which dissolves in a fixed volume of liquid depends on Le Chatelier's Principle.
    Ans. True

24. What occupation is followed by the male suitor in the movie *Meet the Parents*?
    Ans. Nursing

25. How many teeth has a dog: 32, 42, or 52?
    Ans. 42

26. What is the meaning of the Spanish word *humilde*?
    Ans. Humble

27. Give the name of the hot, moist wind which blows from the Sahara to the Iberian Peninsula.
    Ans. The Solano

28. The artists of the Tenebrist School followed the style of which European artist?
    Ans. Caravaggio

29. Who wrote the words for the National Song for use in schools, *I Pledge my Heart*?
    Ans. V.S. Reid

30. Which element has the symbol Pt?
    Ans. Platinum

31. Which football club in England is nicknamed "the Spurs"?
    Ans. Tottenham Hotspurs

32. What name is given to a composition for voices with instrumental or orchestral accompaniment?
    Ans. Cantata

33. How many epistles did St. Paul write?
    Ans. 13

34. Spell the word MISCELLANEOUS.

35. In recent Russian history, what was a gulag?
    Ans. A forced labour prison camp

36. Give the meaning of the French verb *remarquer*.
    Ans. To notice

37. What name is given to a Buddhist priest in Tibet and Mongolia?
    Ans. Lama

38. Which French artist sculptured *The Little Dancer Aged 14*?
    Ans. Degas

39. Which book of the Bible falls between Nahum and Zephaniah?
    Ans. Habakkuk

40. Which Russian revolutionary was born Lev Davidovich Bronstein?
    Ans. Trotsky

III. The Signal Section

Bible Knowledge

1. "Now after the death of Joshua, it came to pass that the children of Israel asked the Lord, saying who shall go up for us against the Canaanites first." This is the first line of which book of the Bible?
    Ans. Judges

Sports

2. What is the maximum weight for a heavyweight in professional boxing?
    Ans. There is no maximum weight limit for heavyweight boxers.

General Knowledge

3. In information technology, what does SIMM mean?
    Ans. Single inline memory module

Biology

4. When Joseph Lister performed his operations in 1865, what did he use to kill bacteria in the air in the operating theatre?
    Ans. Carbolic acid (phenol)

Literature

5. Who wrote the novel *Nicholas Nickleby*?
    Ans. Charles Dickens

Physics

6. A vector is 2 units long and has a component 1.2 units long. What is the other component 90 degrees to the first?
    Ans. 1.6 units

Geography

7. In which country would you find the State of Tamil Nadu?
    Ans. India

Chemistry

8. Place the following metals in order of increasing reactivity: Cu, Ca, Fe.
    Ans. Cu, Fe, Ca

History

9. Which revolutionary founded the National Liberation Guerilla Army in Bolivia in the early 1960s?
    Ans. Che Guevara

English Language

10. Translate into a familiar saying: "Superfluity of culinary artists renders worthless the consommé".
    Ans. Too many cooks spoil the broth.

Music

11. Garfield Vassell was the name given at birth to which Jamaican deejay with an animalistic stage name.
    Ans. Zebra

Jamaican Heritage

12. Which Jamaican secondary school was founded by Jesse Ripoll over 100 years ago?
    Ans. Alpha Academy

Mythology

13. Who was the Roman equivalent to the Greek god of war, Ares?
    Ans. Mars

Mathematics

14. If $y = 1.2 \times 10^3$, what is the value of y^2 in standard form?
    Ans. 1.44×10^6

General Knowledge

15. The chrysanthemum is the imperial flower of which country?
    Ans. Japan

Local and International Affairs

16. In which country would you find the headquarters of UNCTAD?
    Ans. Switzerland

Foreign Languages

17. What phenomenon is denoted by the Spanish *el espectro*?
    Ans. A ghost

Art

18. Which artist has a large painting called *The Garden Party* in the auditorium of the Bank of Jamaica?
    Ans. Barry Watson

Sports

19. Who was Jamaica's first Commonwealth Lightweight boxing champion?
    Ans. Bunny Grant

Biology

20. Limnology is the study of what?
    Ans. Lakes

Geography

21. What is the capital of St. Lucia?
    Ans. Castries

Foreign Languages

22. What is the meaning of the French term *Le Francais d'aujourd'hui*?
    Ans. Today's French

Literature

23. With which biblical character does the hero of Roger Mais' *Black Lightning* show striking similarities?
    Ans. Samson

Theatre and Cinema

24. Which was the first full length feature film made entirely in Jamaica?
    Ans. *The Harder They Come*

Mathematics

25. If $a = 2$, $b = 3$, $c = 5$, what is $\frac{a^6}{b^3c}$?
    Ans. $\frac{64}{135}$

Literature

26. Which West Indian wrote the poem *As John to Patmos*?
    Ans. Derek Walcott

English Language

27. Give a word meaning the headquarters of an army where its stores are kept, of low character, and the lowest part of anything.
    Ans. Base

General Knowledge

28. What name is given to the young of a deer?
    Ans. Fawn

Physics

29. When thorium is bombarded with neutrons, what important nuclear fuel does it change to?
    Ans. Uranium 233

Sports

30. What term in golf denotes the specially prepared surface in which the hole is situated?
    Ans. Green

Chemistry

31. True or false? Sulphur dioxide always acts as an oxidising agent.
    Ans. True

History

32. Name the Secretary-General of the United Nations who died in a plane crash in the Congo in 1961.
    Ans. Dag Hammarsjold

Music

33. Two Jamaicans founded the National Dance Theatre Company. Rex Nettleford was one; who was the other?
    Ans. Eddy Thomas

Jamaican Heritage

34. Which Jamaican journalist and actor do you most associate with the popular "Opportunity Hour" productions from the 1950s?
    Ans. Vere Johns

Biology

35. What is the name given to the emergency procedure used when a piece of food gets stuck in the throat?
    Ans. Tracheoctomy

General Knowledge

36. After how many years of marriage would you celebrate a Pearl anniversary?
    Ans. 30

English Language

37. By adding a prefix, give the opposite of "delicate"?
    Ans. Indelicate

Chemistry

38. What term denotes the energy required for the separation of a formula weight of solid ions into gaseous ions?
    Ans. Lattice energy

Mathematics

39. If $y=2x^2$, and $y^2=144$, what is the positive value of x as a surd in its lowest terms?
    Ans. Root 6

Geography

40. Which is the highest mountain in Africa?
    Ans. Kilamanjaro

Quiz No. 4

I. The Alternate Section

Biology

1. True or false? In the human body, the liver serves primarily in the excretion of waste nitrogen compounds and in regulating the amount of water in the blood.
   Ans. False

2. True or false? Mutations cannot be induced in organisms by exposure to excessive radiation.
   Ans. False

History

3. Identify the king and queen of Spain at the time of Columbus' first voyage.
   Ans. Ferdinand and Isabella

4. In what year did the British Government provide the Negro Education Grant: 1735, 1835 or 1935?
   Ans. 1835

Mathematics

5. What is the image of the point $(5, 4)$ under a reflection in the line $x = 1$?
   Ans. $(^-3, 4)$

6. Find the value of y, if the point $(2, y)$ lies on the line $y = x^3 + 2x^2 + 3$.
   Ans. 19

Art

7. Whom did James Whistler sue in 1878 for describing his painting, *Nocturne in Black and Gold*, as "flinging a pot of paint in the public's face"?
   Ans. Ruskin

8. Name the painter who was the subject of Somerset Maugham's book *The Moon and Sixpence*.
   Ans. Paul Gauguin

Geography

9. What is the term used to describe the removal of unconsolidated material, especially dust, from the surface of the earth by winds?
   Ans. Deflation

10. What term is used to denote the process by which the earth's curved surface is represented on a flat map surface?
    Ans. Map projection

Chemistry

11. An oxide of lead is prepared by heating lead in air at 500 degrees centigrade, followed by treatment with cold concentrated nitric acid. What is the formula of the oxide left: PbO, PbO_2 or Pb_3O_4?
    Ans. PbO_2

12. Which one of the following reagents would completely dissolve an alloy of copper and zinc: (a) dilute HCl, (b) dilute HNO_3, or (c) dilute H_2SO_4?

    Ans. Dilute HNO_3

English Language

13. Give a word ending with the letters "ate" which means to "punish with blows or words, to chastise".

    Ans. Castigate

14. Give a word ending with the letters "ify" which means "to make into a saint" or "to elevate to sainthood".

    Ans. Beatify

Literature

15. Which English poet wrote the famous poem which begins as follows: "Bent double, like old beggars under sacks, Knock-kneed, coughing like hags, we cursed through sludge"?

    Ans. Wilfred Owen

16. Name the poem by W.H. Auden which begins with the line: "He was found by the Bureau of Statistics to be one against whom there was no official complaint"?

    Ans. *The Unknown Citizen*

Foreign Languages

17. If at a university you were in *la faculte de droit*, what would be your area of study?

    Ans. Law

18. State the French word, in English usage, which denotes the re-establishment or recommencement of harmonious relations, especially between States.

    Ans. Rapprochement

Jamaican Heritage

19. Which 17th century landowner in Jamaica was said to have died "with great applause", according to a monument in the Spanish Town Cathedral?

    Ans. Colonel John Colbeck

20. Which Governor of Jamaica declared the Colonial Church Union illegal in 1833?

    Ans. Mulgrave

Literature

21. Which Jamaican wrote the novels *The Painted Canoe*, *The Great Yacht Race* and *The Lunatic*?

    Ans. Anthony Winkler

22. Which West Indian novel by Edgar Mittelholzer is about a strange manuscript said to have magical powers?

    Ans. *My Bones and My Flute*

Local and International Affairs

23. In which Asian country did General Pervez Musharraf stage a coup against Nawaz Sharif to come to power?

    Ans. Pakistan

24. In which European country are the Basque Separatists most active today?

    Ans. Spain

Foreign Languages

25. What is the English equivalent of the Spanish: *Descubrir el pastel*?

    Ans. To let the cat out of the bag; to spill the beans

26. Give the English equivalent of the Spanish proverb: *Al que madruga, Dios le ayuda.*

    Ans. The early bird catches the worm.

Theatre and Cinema

27. Which Jamaican actor played the role of the Superintendent in Kingston in the 1999 movie *Third World Cop*?
    Ans. John Jones

28. Which Jamaican actor played the role of Pa Ben in the first staging of Trevor Rhone's play *Old Story Time* in Jamaica?
    Ans. Charles Hyatt

Mythology

29. In Norse mythology, which son of Odin was the god of poetry?
    Ans. Bragi

30. In Egyptian mythology, Hathor was the sky goddess of love. What form did her head take?
    Ans. That of a cow

History

31. In what year in the decade of the 1970s did Congress start impeachment proceedings against President Nixon?
    Ans. 1974

32. In what year in the decade of the 1970s did the Soweto Uprising take place in South Africa?
    Ans. 1976

Literature

33. In 1888, who completed the first unexpurgated translation of *A Thousand and One Nights*?
    Ans. Sir Richard Burton

34. Give the full title of the novel by Daniel Defoe about Moll Flanders.
    Ans. *The Amorous Adventures of Moll Flanders*

English Language

35. What term is used to describe a sudden descent into the ridiculous or trivial?
    Ans. Bathos, anticlimax

36. Explain the figurative expression "to keep one's nose to the grindstone".
    Ans. To work incessantly

Foreign Languages

37. What is the past participle of the Spanish verb *veer*?
    Ans. *Vesto*

38. What is the meaning of the Spanish *pasar de*?
    Ans. To exceed

Physics

39. A force, F, acting on a body of mass 18 kilograms causes the body to move with an acceleration of 18 metres per second squared. What is the value of F in Newtons?
    Ans. 324 Newtons

40. A force, R, acting on a body of mass 7.5 kilograms causes the body to move with an acceleration of 7.5 metres per second squared. What is the value of R in Newtons?
    Ans. 56.25 Newtons

II. The Speed Section

Speed Questions for Team A

1. Which other Caribbean country gained independence in the same year as Jamaica?
   Ans. Trinidad and Tobago

2. Which Russian composed *Rhapsody on a Theme of Paganini*?
   Ans. Rachmaninov

3. What is the colour of the embroyonic membrane, the placenta?
   Ans. Dark red

4. If the number 33 is multiplied by itself will the result be greater or less than 1000?
   Ans. Greater than 1000

5. Who wrote the novel *Pride and Prejudice*?
   Ans. Jane Austen

6. Spell the word DISASTROUS.

7. Name the Garden on the Mount of Olives where Jesus was betrayed by Judas.
   Ans. Gethsemane

8. What is the French for "the bed"?
   Ans. *Le lit*

9. In which war was the Charge of the Light Brigade?
   Ans. The Crimean War

10. What is the centigrade equivalent of 77 degrees Fahrenheit?
    Ans. 25

11. Which German city is called Aix-la-Chapelle in French?
    Ans. Aachen

12. State the chemical symbol for silver.
    Ans. Ag

13. Which 15th century artist painted *Primavera*?
    Ans. Botticelli

14. Who played the role of Nanny Fine in the television series *The Nanny*?
    Ans. Fran Drescher

15. Give the Spanish phrase for "in a soft voice".
    Ans. *En voz baja*

16. Which novel by Ismith Kahn tells the story of an obeah curse which backfires greatly?
    Ans. *The Jumbie Bird*

17. What term denotes the standard brain wave patterns of a person at rest?
    Ans. Alpha rhythms

18. Which Jamaican place is featured on the back of the $50 note?
    Ans. Doctor's Cave Beach

19. If, on a soda bottle, you saw the abbreviation "fl. oz.", what would this mean?
    Ans. Fluid ounce

20. Which Ugandan leader was overthrown in 1971 by Idi Amin?
    Ans. Milton Obote

21. What term in architecture denotes the main tower of a castle?
    Ans. Keep, or donjon

22. Who won the Wimbledon men's singles title for the year 2002?
    Ans. Lleyton Hewitt

23. In Shakespeare's *The Tempest*, who was the lovely and innocent daughter of Prospero?
    Ans. Miranda

24. What trigonometrical ratio would result if sine A is divided by cosine A?
    Ans. Tangent A

25. In which book of the Bible does Zecharias sing the Benedictus?
    Ans. Luke

26. What is the meaning of the French *l'homme*?
    Ans. The man

27. Which unit of illumination is equal to 1 lumen per square foot?
    Ans. The Foot-candle

28. In ballet, what term denotes bending exercises to loosen up the muscles?
    Ans. Pliés

29. In mythology, who dipped Achilles in the River Styx?
    Ans. Thetis

30. State the Spanish for "the sunset".
    Ans. *El ocaso*

31. Which West Indian has an autobiography in verse, entitled *Another Life*?
    Ans. Derek Walcott

32. In which European city would you find the Spanish Steps?
    Ans. Rome

33. What is the chemical symbol for antimony?
    Ans. Sb

34. Which Jamaican wrote the play *Rosie*?
    Ans. Louis Marriot

35. In what year was John Paul II appointed as Pope?
    Ans. 1978

36. Give the biological name for the breast bone.
    Ans. Sternum

37. Name the male star of the 1998 movie *How Stella Got Her Groove Back*.
    Ans. Taye Diggs

38. Spell the word "ELLIPTICAL".

39. How many hours are there in 1 week?
    Ans. 168

40. What is the Capital of Swaziland?
    Ans. Mbabane

Speed Questions for Team B

1. Which other Caribbean country gained independence in the same year as British Guiana?
   Ans. Barbados

2. Who composed *The Merry Widow* and *The Land of Smiles*?
   Ans. Franz Lehar

3. What is the name of the tenth cranial nerve?
   Ans. Vagus

4. If the number 22 is squared, will the result be greater or less than 500?
   Ans. Less than 500

5. Who wrote the novel *Gone with the Wind*?
   Ans. Margaret Mitchell

6. Spell the word HONOURABLE.

7. According to the New Testament, whom did the crowd prefer to be freed rather than Jesus?
   Ans. Barabbas

8. What is the French for "the window"?
   Ans. *La fenetre*

9. Name the Catholic bishop killed in Rome on February 14, 270 A.D.
   Ans. St. Valentine

10. Give the name of the city overlooked by the Sugar Loaf Mountain.
    Ans. Rio de Janiero

11. State the chemical symbol for gold.
    Ans. Au

12. Which French artist painted *The Rape of the Sabines*?
    Ans. Jacques Louis David

13. State the value of R, the gas constant, to four decimal places.
    Ans. 8.3143 J/K mol

14. Identify the vitamin which prevents pellagra.
    Ans. Niacin or nicotinic acid

15. Which actress played the female lead role in the movie *Rob Roy*?
    Ans. Jessica Lange

16. What is the meaning of the Spanish word *segun*?
    Ans. According to

17. Which West Indian wrote the novel *Season of Adventure*?
    Ans. George Lamming

18. What was the value of a quattie under the pounds, shillings and pence system?
    Ans. $1\frac{1}{2}$ pence

19. If someone is described as a "noodle", what does this mean?
    Ans. He is a simpleton.

20. Which English historian and author wrote the book *The Decline and Fall of the Roman Empire*?
    Ans. Edward Gibbon

21. In art, what is a diptych?
    Ans. A picture painted on two panels

22. Who were the two female finalists at Wimbledon for the year 2002?
    Ans. Venus and Serena Williams

23. In Shakespeare's *Henry V*, whom does Henry marry?
    Ans. Katherine

24. In trigonometry, what is the result when cosine squared A is added to sine squared A?
    Ans. 1

25. Which book of the Bible lies between Ecclesiastes and Isaiah?
    Ans. Song of Solomon

26. In French, who is *un debutant*?
    Ans. A beginner

27. In the formation of the spectrum of white light by a prism, which colour is most deviated?
    Ans. Blue

28. What is another term for counter-tenor in music?
    Ans. Alto

29. In mythology, who carried the spirits of dead warriors to Valhalla?
    Ans. The Valkyries

30. What is an *acantilado* in Spain?
    Ans. A cliff

31. Name the first novel published by Vic Reid.
    Ans. *New Day*

32. In which European city would you find the secretariat or headquarters of NATO?
    Ans. Brussels

33. What is the chemical symbol for mercury.
    Ans. Hg

34. When it was first staged in Jamaica, the dramatic work *Invocation* was performed by one person. Name her.
    Ans. Amina Blackwood Meeks

35. Who preceded Edgerton Clarke as the Roman Catholic Archbishop of Kingston?
    Ans. Samuel Carter

36. Give the biological name for the thigh bone.
    Ans. Femur

37. Name the female star of the 1998 movie *The Avengers*.
    Ans. Uma Thurman

38. Spell the word ANIMOSITY.

39. How many seconds are there in one hour?
    Ans. 3600

40. What is the Capital of Lesotho?
    Ans. Maseru

III. The Signal Section

Biology

1. Give one word for the study of tissues.
   Ans. Histology

Geography

2. What feature is denoted on a map by an equilateral triangle with a dot in its centre?
   Ans. A trigonometrical station

History

3. Name the two British abolitionists who wrote the influential book, *The West Indies in 1837*, concerning the apprenticeship system.
   Ans. Joseph Sturge and Thomas Harvey

Physics

4. An object which appears red absorbs which of the following: (a) red light, (b) green and blue light, (c) blue light, or (d) all of the above?
   Ans. (b) Green and blue light

Bible Knowledge

5. In which city did St. Paul raise Eutychus from the dead?
   Ans. Troas

Literature

6. Which writer, born in St. Kitts but based mainly in Britain and North America, graduated from Oxford University some years before he wrote the novel *Cambridge*?
   Ans. Caryl Phillips

Chemistry

7. What substance is manufactured by the Contact Process?
   Ans. Sulphuric Acid

General Knowledge

8. What is the meaning of the acronym CAPE?
   Ans. Caribbean Advanced Proficiency Examinations

Local and International Affairs

9. The former Police Information Centre in Jamaica is now known by what name?
   Ans. The Constabulary Communications Network

Literature

10. Which literary character was the stepsister of Anastasia and Drizella?
    Ans. Cinderella

Mathematics

11. If $\log_4 16$ is added to $\log_3 81$ and the result is multiplied by the square root of 9, what is the product?
    Ans. 18

Theatre and Cinema

12. Identify the 1966 movie, based on a book by Joy Adamson, in which a Kenyan game warden and his wife must help a lioness make the difficult transition from house pet to wild animal.
    Ans. *Born Free*

Sports

13. What is the name of the netball courts at the National Stadium?
    Ans. The Leila Robinson Courts

English Language

14. According to the saying, it is not over until who sings?
    Ans. The fat lady

General Knowledge

15. Name the African leader, known as "Mwalimu", who visited Jamaica in the 1970s to much acclaim.
    Ans. Julius Nyerere

Proverbs and Idioms

16. Give the meaning of the Jamaican proverb: "John Crow want fe go northside, why you think breeze tek him".
    Ans. Leave the natural order of things alone.

Music

17. Name the song by Monica which scored her first solo number 1 on Billboard's Hot 100 Singles Chart.
    Ans. *The First Night*

History

18. Give the name of the Polish virtuoso pianist and statesman who became Poland's first Prime Minister in 1919.
    Ans. Paderewski

Mathematics

19. Giving your answer in Roman numerals, what does C minus LXXIX equal?
    Ans. XXI

Chemistry

20. What is the chemical formula for chloromethane?
    Ans. CH_3Cl

Art

21. A replica of the Edna Manley work *Rainbow Serpent* is to be found at the Social Science Lecture Theatre at the UWI. Where is the original to be found?
    Ans. At the Little Theatre

Biology

22. To which order do cockroaches belong?
    Ans. Dictyoptera

Literature

23. Which famous lawyer-detective was created by Erle Stanley Garner?
    Ans. Perry Mason

Jamaican Heritage

24. Nanny was considered an Ohemmaa by the Maroons. What does this mean?
    Ans. Female king

Geography

25. On which river does Paris stand?
    Ans. The Seine

History

26. Born Armand Jean du Plessis, he became chief minister of France in 1624, and broke the power of the Huguenots. By what name is he more generally known?
    Ans. Cardinal Richelieu

Sports

27. Name the Hungarian footballer who enjoyed two careers with two of the greatest sides in soccer history, Hungary and Real Madrid. He scored 4 goals in the finals of the 1960 European Cup for Real Madrid.
    Ans. Ferenc Puskas

English Language

28. Distinguish between the words "infer" and "imply".

    Ans. Infer means to conclude or deduce; imply means to hint, mean, or insinuate.

Art

29. Which two areas provided the subject for the paintings produced by Pablo Picasso during his rose period?

    Ans. The theatre and the circus

Religious Knowledge

30. A 13th century theologian undertook to prove that the thoughts of Aristotle were not contrary to Christianity. Who was he?

    Ans. Thomas Aquinas

Mathematics

31. The volume, V, of a cylinder is given. If the radius was doubled, and the height halved, what is the new volume in terms of V?

    Ans. 2V

Foreign Languages

32. Which French term denotes behaviour that is required by etiquette?

    Ans. *De rigueur*

Chemistry

33. When alkanes burn incompletely in air, what three substances may be produced?

    Ans. Carbon dioxide, carbon monoxide and water

Local and International Affairs

34. Which former principal of the Mona Campus of the University of the West Indies received the Norman Manley Award for Excellence in 1998, for his contribution to science in Jamaica?

    Ans. Gerald Lalor

Mythology

35. What punishment was meted out to Prometheus for stealing fire from heaven?

    Ans. He was chained to a mountain while vultures ate his liver.

Physics

36. A ball is thrown upward. What is the acceleration of the ball just before it reaches the top of its flight?

    Ans. $^-9.8 \text{ m/s}^2$

General Knowledge

37. Who was the Italian electrical engineer who, in 1895, invented the first practical system of wireless telegraphy?

    Ans. Guglielmo Marconi

Theatre and Cinema

38. Who is the only person to have won Oscars for best actress and best song?

    Ans. Barbara Streisand

Chemistry

39. What term in chemistry denotes the process in which a regular solid substance is formed from molten mass or from a solution?

    Ans. Crystallization

Literature

40. Name the playwright who wrote *The Wild Duck*.

    Ans. Henrik Ibsen

Quiz No. 5

I. The Alternate Section

General Knowledge

1. Which era in geology covers the last 63 to 64 million years of the Earth's history?
   Ans. Cenozoic

2. Which era preceded the Cenozoic era in the Earth's history?
   Ans. Mesozoic

Theatre and Cinema

3. Which actor played the role of Ben Hur in the 1959 classic movie of the same name?
   Ans. Charlton Heston

4. Which actor played the role of Elmer Gantry in the 1960 movie of the same name?
   Ans. Burt Lancaster

Literature

5. Name the novel by Earl Lovelace which has the characters Fisheye, Terry and Reds.
   Ans. *The Dragon Can't Dance*

6. Name the novel by Jan Carew which has the characters Captain Rhodius and John Pye.
   Ans. *Black Midas*

Sports

7. How many players are there on a men's lacrosse team?
   Ans. 10

8. How many players are there on a women's lacrosse team?
   Ans. 12

Biology

9. Identify the vitamin which prevents pellagra.
   Ans. Niacin or nicotinic acid

10. Identify the vitamin which prevents rickets in children.
    Ans. Vitamin D

Mathematics

11. What is the image of the point (5, 4) under a reflection in the line x = 1?
    Ans. ($^-$3, 4)

12. What is the order of rotational symmetry of an equilateral triangle?
    Ans. 3

History

13. In what year did the Union of South Africa become an independent dominion within the British Empire?
    Ans. 1910

14. In what year was the Dominion of Canada established?
    Ans. 1867

Local and International Affairs

15. In which city would you find the headquarters of the GATT?
    Ans. Geneva

16. In which city would you find the headquarters of UNCTAD?
    Ans. Geneva

Art

17. In art, what is meant by "fresco"?
    Ans. A method of using pigments ground in water applied to a freshly plastered wall or ceiling

18. What name denotes the method of wall-painting in which the wall is first soaked with lime water?
    Ans. Secco painting

Chemistry

19. What is the common name for the substance with the IUPAC name chloroethane?
    Ans. Vinyl chloride

20. What is the common name for the substance with the IUPAC name ethane?
    Ans. Ethane

Physics

21. In physics, what is a rectifier?
    Ans. A device which passes current in only one direction.

22. In physics, what name is given to a rectifier with two diodes?
    Ans. A full wave rectifier

General Knowledge

23. The dong is the unit of currency in which Asian country?
    Ans. Vietnam

24. The leone is the unit of currency in which African country?
    Ans. Sierra Leone

English Language

25. Give a synonym for the word "oriental".
    Ans. Eastern

26. Give a synonym for the word "quondam".
    Ans. Former

Music

27. What term denotes a musical scale of five notes only?
    Ans. Pentatonic Scale

28. Which keys on a piano, black or white, can produce a pentatonic scale?
    Ans. Black

Foreign Languages

29. Give the meaning of the Spanish verb *acercarse*.
    Ans. To approach; to get close

30. Give the meaning of the Spanish verb *irse*.
    Ans. To go away

Jamaican Heritage

31. The famous Bamboo Avenue runs through which sugar estate in St. Elizabeth?
    Ans. The Holland Sugar Estate

32. On a visit to Jamaica in 1966, the Queen opened the new Town Centre in which rural capital?
    Ans. Lucea

Literature

33. This French Romantic writer opposed Napoleon III as Emperor and spent 19 years in exile. His works include the play *Ruy Bas*. Name him.
    Ans. Victor Hugo

34. Identify the Greek tragic playwright whose plays include *Medea* and *The Trojan Women*.
    Ans. Euripides

Religious Knowledge

35. Which is the fourth largest religion in India, located mainly in the Punjab?
    Ans. Sikhism

36. Name the founder of Sikhism.
    Ans. Nanak

Foreign Languages

37. What type of shop is *la charcuterie* in France?
    Ans. A pork butcher's shop

38. What type of building is *le chateau en sable* in France?
    Ans. A sandcastle

General Knowledge

39. Which African country's name means "The Land of Honest People"?
    Ans. Burkina Faso

40. Which African country's name means "The Mountain of the Lion"?
    Ans. Sierra Leone

II. The Speed Section

Speed Questions for Team A

1. Name the director of the movie *Dances With Wolves*.
   Ans. Kevin Costner

2. What is $\frac{1}{4}$ of $\frac{1}{8}$?
   Ans. $\frac{1}{32}$

3. How many players are there on an American football team?
   Ans. 11

4. Which West Indian wrote the book *Party Politics in the West Indies* in 1962?
   Ans. C.L.R. James

5. According to legend, an Arawak Indian at which part of Jamaica begged Columbus to take him to their country?
   Ans. Montego Bay

6. Is Shintoism a version of Hinduism, Sikhism or Buddhism?
   Ans. Buddhism

7. In what year did the Battle of Tsushima take place?
   Ans. 1905

8. Name the stage between the larva and the adult in the development of the insect.
   Ans. Pupa

9. Give a word denoting the region near or towards the head of an animal.
   Ans. Anterior

10. State the centigrade equivalent of 50 degrees Fahrenheit.
    Ans. 10 degrees centigrade

11. What is the value of the acceleration due to gravity to five decimal places.
    Ans. 9.80665 m/s^2

12. Explain the figurative expression "Elysian happiness".
    Ans. A state of perfect bliss

13. Which female voice is between contralto and soprano?
    Ans. Mezzo-soprano

14. What is the past participle of the Spanish verb *decir*?
    Ans. *Dicho*

15. Give the meaning of the French verb *se lever*.
    Ans. To get up

16. Which is the most recently formed of Jamaica's parishes?
    Ans. Manchester

17. Which West Indian wrote the novel *In a Free State*?
    Ans. V.S. Naipaul

18. What is the value of $\frac{2}{3}$ divided by $\frac{1}{4}$?
    Ans. $\frac{8}{3}$

19. In geography, what is a dyke?
    Ans. A vertical or steeply inclined sheet of magma which has solidified underground.

20. Who won the Best Actor Oscar in 1984 for his performance in the movie *Amadeus*?
    Ans. F. Murray Abraham

21. Who was the chief editor of the French *Encyclopedie*?
    Ans. Denis Diderot

22. Which female tennis player was the first winner of the Grand Slam?
    Ans. Maureen Connolly

23. What is the unit of currency in Haiti?
    Ans. Gourde

24. Which English artist designed the tapestry *Christ in Glory* for the Coventry Cathedral?
    Ans. Graham Sutherland

25. Are the Vedas holy books in the Buddhist or Hindu religion?
    Ans. The Hindu religion

26. In what year did the Battle of the Nile take place?
    Ans. 1798

27. To which phylum do starfish belong?
    Ans. Echinodermata

28. Which has the longer average lifespan: a bear or a rabbit?
    Ans. Bear

29. What is the atomic number of copper?
    Ans. 29

30. Which metal has an ore known as celestine?
    Ans. Strontium

31. Complete the proverb: "Every man for himself ..."
    Ans. "... and God for us all."

32. Which American composer wrote the musical *Call Me Madam*?
    Ans. Irvine Berlin

33. Give the Spanish for "the thermometer".
    Ans. *El termometro*

34. What is the meaning of the French *tout le monde*?
    Ans. Everybody

35. How many cubes, each with sides 2 cubic centimetres, can fit into a cube with sides 8 cubic centimetres in length?
    Ans. 64

36. In art, what is meant by "nimbus"?
    Ans. The halo or disc surrounding the head of a religious figure

37. State the plural of the word "custos".
    Ans. Custodes

38. Which Englishman wrote the play *The Constant Wife*?
    Ans. W. Somerset Maugham

39. What is the SI unit of capacitance?
    Ans. The farad

40. Give the meaning of the acronym OPEC.
    Ans. Organization of Petroleum Exporting Countries

Speed Questions for Team B

1. Name the director of the movie *Born on the 4th of July*.
   Ans. Oliver Stone

2. What is $\frac{1}{5}$ of $\frac{1}{5}$?
   Ans. $\frac{1}{25}$

3. How many players are there on an Australian Rules Football team?
   Ans. 18

4. Who wrote the book *My Mother Who Fathered Me*?
   Ans. Edith Clarke

5. According to legend, an Arawak Indian at which part of Jamaica begged Columbus to take him to their country?
   Ans. Montego Bay

6. Shintoism was disestablished in 1945 when which Japanese Emperor renounced his divine powers?
   Ans. Hirohito

7. In what year did the Battle of the Somme take place?
   Ans. 1916

8. What is an organelle?
   Ans. A body in a cell that has a specialized function

9. Give a word meaning "of or close to the back of an animal".
   Ans. Dorsal

10. State the centigrade equivalent of 59 degrees Fahrenheit.
    Ans. 15 degrees centigrade

11. What is the value of e, the base of natural logarithms.
    Ans. 2.71828

12. Explain the figurative expression "to fall through".
    Ans. To fail

13. What is the meaning of the musical term *legato*?
    Ans. One note leading smoothly to the next

14. What is the past participle of the Spanish verb *oir*?
    Ans. *Oido*

15. Give the meaning of the French verb *attirer*.
    Ans. To attract

16. In what year was the parish of Manchester formed?
    Ans. 1814

17. Which West Indian wrote the novel *Green Days By the River*?
    Ans. Michael Anthony

18. What is the value of $\frac{2}{5}$ divided by 8?
    Ans. $\frac{1}{20}$

19. In geography, what is an erg?
    Ans. A desert covered by sand dunes

20. Who won the Best Actor Oscar in 1985 for his performance in the movie *Kiss of the Spider Woman*?
    Ans. William Hurt

21. Name the author of the book *August 1914*.
    Ans. Alexander Solzhenitsyn

22. Who is the only man to have led the world in both tennis and table tennis?
    Ans. Fred Perry

23. What is the unit of currency in Greece?
    Ans. Euro

24. Which artist painted *Elevation of the Cross*, for the Antwerp Cathedral?
    Ans. Peter Paul Rubens

25. How many holy books constitute the Vedas?
    Ans. 4

26. In what year did the Battle of Austerlitz take place?
    Ans. 1805

27. To which phylum do moss animals belong?
    Ans. Bryozoans

28. Which has the longer average lifespan: an elephant or a dog?
    Ans. Elephant

29. What is the atomic number of gold?
    Ans. 79

30. Which metal has an ore known as rock salt?
    Ans. Sodium

31. Complete the proverb: "Do not count your chickens ..."
    Ans. "... before they are hatched."

32. Which American musician wrote the score for the musical *West Side Story*?
    Ans. Leonard Bernstein

33. Give the Spanish for "the cream" or "ointment".
    Ans. *La crema*

34. What is the French word meaning "thus"?
    Ans. *Ainsi*

35. How many cubes, each with sides 3 centimetres in length, can fit into a cube with sides 6 centimetres?
    Ans. 8

36. What term denotes the technique of painting with colours that have been mixed with water soluble gum?
    Ans. Water colour

37. Give both plural forms of the word "index".
    Ans. Indices and indexes

38. Which Frenchman wrote the novel *Emile*?
    Ans. Jean Jacques Rousseau

39. What is the SI unit of illuminance?
    Ans. The lux

40. Give the meaning of the abbreviation OAU.
    Ans. Organization of African Unity

III. The Signal Section

Geography

1. In which African country would you find Mount Iboundji, the town of Lambarene, and the city of Libreville?
   Ans. Gabon

Theatre and Cinema

2. For her performance in which movie did Cher win the Best Actress Oscar in 1987?
   Ans. *Moonstruck*

General Knowledge

3. In 1733–34, who wrote a famous *Essay on Man*?
   Ans. Alexander Pope

Sports

4. Which tennis player was known as "Little Miss Poker Face"?
   Ans. Helen Wills Moody

Art

5. Identify the English sculptor, and advocate of direct carving, who is best known for his reclining figures.
   Ans. Henry Moore

Religious Knowledge

6. What term denotes the 9th month of the year in Islam?
   Ans. Ramadan

Biology

7. True or false? A monoecious plant has only male flowers.
   Ans. False

Chemistry

8. Whose law states that the weight of gas dissolved by a liquid is proportional to the gas pressure?
   Ans. Henry's

History

9. Give the name of the British liner which was sunk by a German U-boat in 1915, causing many civilian casualties.
   Ans. The Lusitania

English Language

10. Explain the figurative expression "Fabian tactics".
    Ans. A policy of wearing down an opponent by delaying action

Jamaican Heritage

11. Which French refugee, in a will of 1764, left all his real and personal estate for the establishment of a free school in Hanover?
    Ans. Martin Rusea

Chemistry

12. Which metal has an ore known as stibnite?
    Ans. Antimony

Literature

13. Which West Indian wrote the short stories in the book *Gingertown*?
    Ans. Claude McKay

Mathematics

14. Which is larger 2^{-2} or $(\frac{1}{4})^2$?
    Ans. 2^{-2}

Foreign Languages

15. Give the meaning of the Spanish term *suavemente*.
    Ans. Gently

Music

16. Which Jamaican entertainer was given the name Calvin Scott at birth?
    Ans. Cocoa Tea

Geography

17. Which African city's name means "Haven of Peace"?
    Ans. Dar Es Salaam

Literature

18. Which British poet is known mainly for his translation of *The Rubaiyat of Omar Khayyam*?
    Ans. Edward Fitzgerald

Foreign Languages

19. State two meanings for the French word *toujours*.
    Ans. Always; still

Jamaican Heritage

20. Fort Charlotte is named in honour of George III's queen. In which Jamaican town is it located?
    Ans. Lucea

Physics

21. In the formula W = hv, where h is Planck's Constant, what is W?
    Ans. Energy of a quantum

History

22. Which British historian and statesman wrote *History of England*, covering 1685 to 1702?
    Ans. Thomas Macaulay

Chemistry

23. Name the element which was once known as eka-aluminium.
    Ans. Gallium

Mathematics

24. Evaluate cos 45 over sin 60.
    Ans. $\frac{2}{\sqrt{6}}$

English Language

25. Give a word ending with the letters "ate" which means to cause to begin.
    Ans. Originate; initiate

General Knowledge

26. The winner of the Nobel Prize for Literature in 1929 opposed Nazism and went into exile. Name him.
    Ans. Thomas Mann

Literature

27. Name the only novel written by C.L.R. James.
    Ans. *Minty Alley*

Biology

28. True or false? The ovule of a seed-bearing plant contains the egg cell.
    Ans. True

Foreign Languages

29. Give the meaning of the Spanish verb *casarse*.
    Ans. To get married

Geography

30. Plymouth is the capital of which Caribbean island?
    Ans. Montserrat

Local and International Affairs

31. Who preceded Kofi Annan as the Secretary-General of the United Nations?
    Ans. Boutros Boutros Ghali

Chemistry

32. How many molecules of water of crystallization are there in crystalline sodium sulphate, also known as Glauber's salt?
    Ans. 10

Foreign Languages

33. What is the French word meaning "starving"?
    Ans. *Affame*

Religious Knowledge

34. What term denotes the festival of the Jewish New Year?
    Ans. Rosh Hashanah

General Knowledge

35. Born 1847, died 1922, this Scottish-American invented the telephone. Name him.
    Ans. Alexander Graham Bell

History

36. In what year did the West Indies Federation come to an end?
    Ans. 1961

Mathematics

37. What is the area of a circle with radius 7 centimetres?
    Ans. 154 square centimetres

Music

38. Which German composer wrote the *Moonlight Sonata*?
    Ans. Beethoven

Chemistry

39. Which element has the greater atomic number: manganese or mercury?
    Ans. Mercury

English Language

40. Give the meaning of the figurative expression "Dutch courage".
    Ans. Bravery induced by alcohol

Quiz No. 6

I. The Alternate Section

Geography

1. What term denotes the type of lava which, when it solidifies, has a rough and jagged surface?
   Ans. Aa

2. What term denotes a layer of rock through which ground water percolates?
   Ans. Aquifer

Theatre and Cinema

3. For his performance in which film did Anthony Hopkins win the Best Actor Oscar in 1991?
   Ans. *The Silence of the Lambs*

4. For her performance in which film did Jodie Foster win the Best Actress Oscar in 1988?
   Ans. *The Accused*

Literature

5. Name the Italian poet and diplomat who wrote *Orlando Furioso*.
   Ans. Ludovico Ariosto

6. He was the greatest Greek comedy writer, and his work includes *The Wasps*. Name him.
   Ans. Aristophanes

Sports

7. Who captained the English football team which won the World Cup in 1966?
   Ans. Bobby Moore

8. Which American won the world middleweight title five times, and was world champion in the welterweight division as well?
   Ans. Sugar Ray Robinson

General Knowledge

9. What is the unit of currency in Nicaragua?
   Ans. Cordoba

10. What is the unit of currency in Peru?
    Ans. Sol

Art

11. What French term denotes the freest form of action painting in which accidental patterns are produced by applying paint to any surface in any way at all?
    Ans. *Tachisme* (French for stain or blot)

12. Who was the pioneer of *Tachisme*?
    Ans. Dubuffet

General Knowledge

13. In which city is there an annual Caribana parade commemorating Caribbean culture?
    Ans. Toronto

14. In which city is there an annual Caribbean carnival at Notting Hill?
    Ans. London

Chemistry

15. Which has the higher atomic number: barium or aluminium?
    Ans. Barium

16. Which has the higher atomic number: fluorine or iodine?
    Ans. Iodine

Physics

17. State the centigrade equivalent of 77 degrees Fahrenheit.
    Ans. 25 degrees centigrade

18. State the centigrade equivalent of 95 degrees Fahrenheit.
    Ans. 35 degrees centigrade

History

19. In what century did Muhammad found the Islam faith?
    Ans. 7th century

20. In what century was the Jehovah's Witness Movement founded?
    Ans. 19th century

Foreign Languages

21. Give the meaning of the Spanish verb *levatarse*.
    Ans. To get up

22. Give the meaning of the Spanish verb *cansarse*.
    Ans. To get tired

Mathematics

23. Factorize $2x^2 - 2x - 4$.
    Ans. $(2x + 2)(x - 2)$

24. Factorize $3x^2 + 4x + 1$.
    Ans. $(3x + 1)(x + 1)$

General Knowledge

25. Give a three-lettered term which denotes an informal written promise to pay a sum of money owed to another.
    Ans. IOU

26. What term in economics denotes the money borrowed by a government from individuals and institutions to pay for expenditure that cannot be covered from ordinary revenue?
    Ans. National debt

English Language

27. What is the meaning of the word "hamate"?
    Ans. Crooked

28. What is the meaning of the word "desuetude"?
    Ans. Disuse

History

29. Name the first of the Frankish kings.
    Ans. Charlemagne

30. Name the first of the Saxon kings.
    Ans. Henry I, the Fowler

Biology

31. To which order do true bugs belong?
    Ans. Hemiptera

32. To which order do biting lice belong?
    Ans. Mallophaga

Music

33. What term in music denotes unaccompanied singing in free rhythm, as used in church services?
    Ans. Chanting

34. What term in music denotes a vocal work, typically for soloists, a chorus or the orchestra?
    Ans. Cantata

Foreign Languages

35. What kind of ticket is *un aller et retour* in France?
    Ans. A return ticket

36. What type of association is *L'Association de Parents d'Eleves* in France?
    Ans. Parent Teachers' Association

Jamaican Heritage

37. In Jamaica's history, there was a flourishing trade in which type of timber in Black River?
    Ans. Logwood

38. The Parish Church of St. John the Evangelist in Black River contains a monument to Robert Hugh Munro and Caleb Dickson. Who made it?
    Ans. Henry Westmacott

West Indian Literature

39. In which story by Samuel Selvon would you find the characters Rockabye and Teena?
    Ans. *Brackley and the Bed*

40. In which story by Jean Rhys would you find the characters Eddie and the Sawyers?
    Ans. *The Day They Burned The Books*

II. The Speed Section

Speed Questions for Team A

1. On the Beaufort Scale, what number symbolises a moderate gale?
    Ans. 7

2. Who won the Best Actor Oscar in 1981?
    Ans. Henry Fonda

3. Name the author of *Who's Afraid of Virginia Wolf.*
    Ans. Edward Albee

4. What is the nationality of the former long distance runner Henry Rono?
    Ans. Kenyan

5. What is the unit of currency in Lesotho?
    Ans. The Rand

6. True or false? The diagonals of a square are of equal length.
    Ans. True

7. In what century did the Rococo art style flourish?
    Ans. 18th (1735–1765)

8. What term denotes minted coins as opposed to notes or bills in business?
    Ans. Specie

9. What name is given to the Islamic official who conducts the prayers of a mosque?
    Ans. Imam

10. Who shot Robert Kennedy?
    Ans. Sirhan Sirhan

11. To which phylum do jellyfish belong?
    Ans. Coelenterata

12. What is the atomic number of argon?
    Ans. 18

13. State the speed of light in metres per second.
    Ans. 2.997925×10^8 m/s

14. Who or what is a mendicant?
    Ans. A beggar

15. Which male voice is higher than bass and lower than tenor?
    Ans. Baritone

16. What is the past participle of the Spanish verb *andar*?
    Ans. *Andado*

17. Give the meaning of the French verb *briller*.
    Ans. To shine

18. Which is the largest parish in Jamaica?
    Ans. St. Elizabeth

19. Which West Indian wrote the novel *Black Albino*?
    Ans. Namba Roy

20. If the tangent of an angle is $\frac{5}{12}$, what is the cosine of the same angle?
    Ans. $\frac{12}{13}$

21. Who was the Biblical mother of Joseph?
    Ans. Rachel

22. Which Jamaican musician was given the name Keith Anderson at birth?
   Ans. Bob Andy

23. Which Central American country has Tajumulco as its highest point?
   Ans. Guatemala

24. Name the director of the movie *The Unforgiven*.
   Ans. Clint Eastwood

25. Which American wrote the novel *The Turn of the Screw*?
   Ans. Henry James

26. What is the unit of currency in Nigeria?
   Ans. The naira

27. In art, what is a triptych?
   Ans. A series of three painted panels or doors that are hinged or folded.

28. Is Jainism an offshoot of Hinduism or Judaism?
   Ans. Hinduism

29. Who served as British Prime Minister for one year between 1964 and 1965?
   Ans. Sir Alec Douglas-Home

30. Is ringworm caused by fungi or bacteria?
   Ans. Fungi

31. State the IUPAC name for butylene.
   Ans. Butene

32. Which is the lightest of all solid elements?
   Ans. Lithium

33. Complete the proverb: "Give a dog a bad name ..."
   Ans. "... and hang him."

34. What term in music denotes an absence of a sense of key?
   Ans. Atonality

35. In Spanish, who is *el vaquero*?
   Ans. A cowboy

36. What is the meaning of the French verb *contenir*?
   Ans. To contain

37. On which river is the town of May Pen located?
   Ans. The Rio Minho

38. What fraction of a revolution is 9 degrees?
   Ans. $\frac{1}{40}$

39. In which Caribbean city is Woodford Square located?
   Ans. Port of Spain

40. Which West Indian wrote *Spratt Morrison*?
   Ans. Jean DaCosta

Speed Questions for Team B

1. On the Beaufort Scale, what number symbolises a light air?
   Ans. 1

2. Who won the Best Actress Oscar in 1981?
   Ans. Katherine Hepburn

3. Who wrote the fairy tale *The Red Shoes*?
   Ans. Hans Christian Andersen

4. What was the nationality of the former tennis player Suzanne Lenglen?
   Ans. French

5. What is the unit of currency in Mexico?
   Ans. The peso

6. True or false? The diagonals of a rectangle are of equal length.
   Ans. True

7. In what century did the Baroque style first come to prominence?
   Ans. 16th (1500s to 1700s)

8. In economics, give another term for a slump.
   Ans. A depression

9. In religious knowledge, what was the hegira?
   Ans. The flight of Muhammad from Mecca to Medina in 622 A.D.

10. Who shot John F. Kennedy?
    Ans. Lee Harvey Oswald

11. To which phylum do sponges belong?
    Ans. Porifera

12. What is the atomic number of arsenic?
    Ans. 33

13. State the value of the gravitational constant.
    Ans. 6.670×10^{-11} N m^2/kg^2

14. Who or what is a pugilist?
    Ans. A boxer

15. Which is the first note on the musical scale?
    Ans. Tonic

16. What is the past participle of the Spanish verb *conducir*?
    Ans. *Conducido*

17. Give the meaning of the French verb *comprendre*.
    Ans. To understand

18. Other than Kingston, which is the smallest parish in Jamaica?
    Ans. Hanover

19. Which West Indian wrote the novel *Natives of My Person*?
    Ans. George Lamming

20. If the sine of an angle is $\frac{10}{25}$, what is the tangent of the same angle?
    Ans. $\frac{10}{24}$

21. Who was the Biblical mother of Jacob?
    Ans. Rebekah

22. Which Jamaican entertainer was given the name Clifton Bailey at birth?
    Ans. Capleton

23. Which Middle Eastern country has Mount Meron as its highest point?
    Ans. Israel

24. Name the director of the movie *The Silence of the Lambs*.
    Ans. Jonathan Demme

25. Which English author wrote the novel *Adam Bede*?
    Ans. George Eliot

26. What is the unit of currency in Egypt?
    Ans. The pound

27. What name denotes a series of painted doors or panels with more parts than a triptych?
    Ans. Polyptych

28. Is the Talmud associated with Judaism or Islam?
    Ans. Judaism

29. Who served as British Prime Minister from 1970 to 1974?
    Ans. Edward Heath

30. Is measles caused by a virus or a bacterium?
    Ans. Virus

31. State the IUPAC name for Butyl alcohol.
    Ans. Butanol

32. Which has the higher specific gravity: alcohol or water?
    Ans. Water

33. Complete the proverb: "Experience keeps a dear school ..."
    Ans. "... but fools will learn in no other."

34. What term in music denotes the decoration of basic notes of a melody?
    Ans. Ornament

35. In Spanish, what is *la guerra*?
    Ans. War

36. What is the meaning of the French word *comment*?
    Ans. How

37. In which Jamaican parish would you find Milk River?
    Ans. Clarendon

38. What fraction of a revolution is 72 degrees?
    Ans. $\frac{1}{5}$

39. In which Caribbean city would you find Trafalgar Square?
    Ans. Bridgetown

40. Which West Indian wrote *Beyond the Boundary*?
    Ans. C.L.R. James

III. The Signal Section

Geography

1. In geography, what term denotes an area from which a river or reservoir draws its water supply?
    Ans. Catchment area (or drainage area)

Theatre and Cinema

2. Who won the Best Actor Oscar for his performance in the movie *Judgment at Nuremberg* in 1961?
    Ans. Maximilian Schnell

General Knowledge

3. He was a Greek philosopher, and his work includes *The Ethics*. Name him.
    Ans. Aristotle

Sports

4. Which cricketer held the record for the highest individual test innings before it was broken by Brian Lara?
    Ans. Sir Garfield Sobers

Art

5. Which group of mid-19th century French landscape painters included Corot, Millet and Rousseau?
    Ans. The Barbizon School

Religious Knowledge

6. In Buddhism and Hinduism, what is the doctrine that a man's deeds determine his destiny?
    Ans. Karma

Biology

7. Which organ of the body is affected by emphysema?
    Ans. Lung

Physics

8. True or false? Delta rays are electrons knocked out of atoms by low energy charged particles.
    Ans. False

English Language

9. Spell the word ECCENTRIC.

Music

10. Who composed *The St. Matthew Passion*?
    Ans. Johann Sebastian Bach

Chemistry

11. Which has the higher atomic number: iron or mercury?
    Ans. Mercury

Spanish

12. What is the Spanish for "the remedy".
    Ans. *El remedio*

Geography

13. In which Jamaican parish is the town of Middle Quarters?
    Ans. St. Elizabeth

General Knowledge

14. In insurance, what is a whole life policy?
    Ans. One that matures only upon death.

History

15. Who succeeded Dwight Eisenhower as American President in 1961?
    Ans. John F. Kennedy

Literature

16. Born in British Guiana in 1921, his books include *Age of the Rainmakers* and *Black Marsden*. Name him.
    Ans. Wilson Harris

Mathematics

17. Evaluate the 10th term of the series 2, 6, 10, 14.
    Ans. 38

Religious Knowledge

18. Give the meaning of the religious word paschal.
    Ans. Relating to Passover or to Easter

General Knowledge

19. What term denotes an economic system in which there is minimum government interference?
    Ans. Laissez-faire

Foreign Languages

20. Give the meaning of the French term *se trouver*.
    Ans. To be situated

Physics

21. True or false? Below the critical temperature a gas cannot be liquefied, no matter how great the pressure.
    Ans. False

Geography

22. In geography, what term denotes a deep, steep-sided crater in the top of a volcano?
    Ans. Crater

Biology

23. Which organ of the body is affected by pyelitis?
    Ans. The kidney

Chemistry

24. What is the chemical symbol for the element manganese?
    Ans. Mn

Religious Knowledge

25. In which two parts of the world are Buddhists priests known as Lamas?
    Ans. Tibet and Mongolia

Foreign Languages

26. What is the Spanish for the chemist's shop.
    Ans. *La farmacia*

Literature

27. Name the French playwright who wrote *The Ring Round the Moon*.
    Ans. Jean Anouilh

General Knowledge

28. The kwacha is the unit of currency in which African country?
    Ans. Malawi

English Language

29. State the opposite of the word opaque.
    Ans. Transparent

Music

30. How many passions did Johann Sebastian Bach compose?
    Ans. 3

Art

31. Which group of British painters of the 1950s included David Bomberg and John Bratby?
    Ans. Kitchen Sink School

Foreign Languages

32. Give the meaning of the French term *a toute vitesse*.
    Ans. At top speed

Geography

33. What is the capital of St. Lucia?
    Ans. Castries

Literature

34. Identify the West Indian who has an anthology of poems entitled *Jamaica Labrish*.
    Ans. Louise Bennett

Mathematics

35. What is the area of a square field if its perimeter is 32 metres?
    Ans. 64 square metres

Religious Knowledge

36. Name the Greek word for the coming of Christ at the end of history.
    Ans. Parousia

History

37. The phrase "Liberty, Equality, Fraternity" was most associated with which 18th century European Revolution?
    Ans. The French Revolution

Physics

38. Who discovered the proton, in 1919?
    Ans. Ernest Rutherford

Biology

39. Is German measles caused by a virus or a bacterium?
    Ans. Virus

Local and International Affairs

40. Give the meaning of the acronym NATO.
    Ans. North Atlantic Treaty Organization

Quiz No. 7

I. The Alternate Section

Bible Knowledge

1. Name the parents of King Solomon.
   Ans. David and Bathsheba

2. Name the two sons of Jacob and Rachel.
   Ans. Joseph and Benjamin

General Knowledge

3. In which European city would you find the Spanish Steps?
   Ans. Rome

4. The smallest country in the world has an area of just over 100 acres. Name it.
   Ans. The Vatican City

Foreign Languages

5. Give the meaning of the Spanish *el trabajo*.
   Ans. Work, task, trouble

6. Give the meaning of the Spanish *el vaquero*.
   Ans. Cowboy, herdsman

Mathematics

7. If x is equal to the square root of y, and y is equal to the square root of 256, what are the two possible values of y?
   Ans. 4, ⁻4

8. If y is inversely proportional to x, and y is equal to four when x is one-half, what is the value of y when x is 6?
   Ans. $\frac{1}{3}$

Literature

9. Which West Indian wrote the novel *Season of Adventure*?
   Ans. George Lamming

10. Which West Indian wrote the novel *King of the Masquerade*?
    Ans. Michael Anthony

Biology

11. What term denotes the standard brain wave patterns of a person at rest?
    Ans. Alpha rhythms

12. What term denotes the brain spaces filled with cerebro-spinal fluid?
    Ans. Ventricles

Chemistry

13. True or false? Reduction always occurs when non-metallic ions become ions.
    Ans. False

14. True or false? Reduction always occurs at the cathode in any electrolytic process.
    Ans. True

English Language

15. Give the meaning of the figurative expression "rough and ready".

     Ans. Hastily prepared; without neatness or adornment

16. Give the meaning of the figurative expression "rough and tumble".

     Ans. In a disorderly manner

History

17. Name the Russian-born research chemist who became the first president of Israel in 1948.

     Ans. Chaim Weizmann

18. Name the pianist who became the first president of Poland in 1919.

     Ans. Ignace Paderewski

Physics

19. The relative density of an oil is 0.9. What is the mass of 18 cm³ of the oil?

     Ans. 16.2 grams

20. The relative density of an oil is 0.9. What is the volume of 27 grams of the oil?

     Ans. 30 cm³

Theatre and Cinema

21. Which movie, about a country's independence leader, won the Academy Award for Best Film in 1982?

     Ans. *Gandhi*

22. Which movie, about British athletics, won the Academy Award for Best Film in 1981?

     Ans. *Chariots of Fire*

Jamaican Heritage

23. In which Jamaican parish did the insurrection led by Tacky take place?

     Ans. St. Mary

24. In what year did the insurrection led by Tacky take place?

     Ans. 1760

Geography

25. What is the capital of Tajikistan?

     Ans. Dushanbe

26. What is the capital of Tuvalu?

     Ans. Funafuti

Biology

27. Which of the following drugs does not have a major effect on the central nervous system: valium, aspirin or alcohol?

     Ans. Aspirin

28. Which of the following parts controls the amount of light entering the eye: cornea, pupil or iris?

     Ans. Iris

Foreign Languages

29. Give the meaning of the French term *a la recherche de*.

     Ans. In search of

30. Give the meaning of the French term *faire les bagages*.

     Ans. To pack

Literature

31. Name the Jesuit priest, an outstanding name in 19th century poetry, whose work was not published until 1918.

     Ans. Gerald Manley Hopkins

32. Name the 19th to 20th century Irish dramatist, a lifelong socialist and reformist, who began his career as a music and drama critic.

     Ans. George Bernard Shaw

Art

33. Which artist was court painter to Charles I?

    Ans. Van Dyck

34. Which 19th century French artist was mainly concerned with portraying peasant life?

    Ans. Millet

Sports

35. Identify the former Trinidadian cricketer who was knighted and later became a member of the British House of Lords.

    Ans. Learie Constantine

36. Identify the former Guyanese cricketer who became a Government minister in his country.

    Ans. Roy Fredericks

Jamaican Heritage

37. With which field of activity in Jamaica do you most associate the name Beth Jacobs?

    Ans. Family planning

38. With what field of activity in Jamaica do you most associate the name R.O.C. King?

    Ans. Religion

Physics

39. How many joules of thermal energy are supplied by a 1 kilowatt heater in 12 minutes?

    Ans. 720,000 J

40. How many joules of thermal energy are supplied by a 1 kilowatt heater in 15 minutes?

    Ans. 900,000 J

II. The Speed Section

Speed Questions for Team A

1. Which book of the Bible lies between Nehemiah and Job?
   Ans. Esther

2. Which Jamaican sang *Shy Guy*, the title song for the movie *Bad Boys*?
   Ans. Diana King

3. True or false? Sulphur is polymorphic.
   Ans. True

4. Give a word ending in "ate" which means to surrender to an enemy on agreed terms.
   Ans. Capitulate

5. Which French Revolutionary leader spearheaded the Reign of Terror?
   Ans. Robespierre

6. Name the Roman deity depicted with two faces.
   Ans. Janus

7. Which two eye defects are likely to be corrected by bifocal lenses?
   Ans. Myopia and presbyopia

8. What is the capital of Algeria?
   Ans. Algiers

9. Which of the following does not have a tetrahedral shape: CH_4, CO_2, or NH_4?
   Ans. CO_2

10. The first novel of this Polish-born sea captain was *Almayer's Folly*. Name him.
    Ans. Joseph Conrad

11. Who composed the opera *La Boheme*?
    Ans. Puccini

12. Whose law in physics states the relationship between the velocity of diffusion of a gas and its density?
    Ans. Graham's Law

13. In which country is there a news agency known as ITAR-TASS?
    Ans. Russia

14. In which Jamaican mountain range is Nanny Town located?
    Ans. The Blue Mountains

15. What is the next prime number after 71?
    Ans. 73

16. A lens has a focal distance of 400 mm. What is the power of the lens in dioptres?
    Ans. 2.5D

17. What is the nationality of the footballer Jurgen Klinsman?
    Ans. German

18. Who discovered the circulation of the blood?
    Ans. William Harvey

19. Which crop in the Caribbean is affected by the berry borer pest?
    Ans. Coffee

20. Which English king was known as the Merry Monarch?
    Ans. Charles II

21. What property of an object is given by the formula heat energy divided by mass?
    Ans. Specific latent heat

22. In *My Fair Lady*, who taught Eliza Doolittle to be a lady?
    Ans. Professor Henry Higgins

23. Round off 10.8272 to the nearest hundredth?
    Ans. 10.83

24. In which Caribbean colony did Governor Barkly serve during the mid-nineteenth century?
    Ans. Guyana

25. Give the meaning of the Spanish verb *estacionar*.
    Ans. To park

26. Which Jamaican entertainer had the hit song *Lord, Give Me Strength*?
    Ans. Luciano

27. Cinnabar is an ore of which metal?
    Ans. Mercury

28. Which West Indian wrote the short stories in the book *Gingertown*?
    Ans. Claude McKay

29. Which pigment mainly determines skin colour?
    Ans. Melanin

30. Who first conceived the idea of using lines of force to represent magnetic fields: Ampere, Faraday or Fleming?
    Ans. Faraday

31. Give the meaning of the abbreviation ACS in international affairs.
    Ans. Association of Caribbean States

32. What is 0.64 divided by 8?
    Ans. 0.08

33. Spell the word ABSENTEEISM.

34. In which African country is the town of Arusha located: Tanzania, Zaire or Ghana?
    Ans. Tanzania

35. Name the theatre in London which opened in the 16th century with performances by Lord Chamberlain's Men.
    Ans. The Globe Theatre

36. Which pre-Raphaelite artist painted *The Death of Ophelia*?
    Ans. John Millais

37. State the chemical formula for chloroform.
    Ans. $CHCl_3$

38. Which political party in Guyana is abbreviated as the PNC?
    Ans. People's National Congress

39. The mean of two numbers is 82. If one number is 90, what is the other?
    Ans. 74

40. What important vitamin is found in carrots?
    Ans. Vitamin A

Speed Questions for Team B

1. Which book of the Bible lies between Lamentations and Daniel?
   Ans. Ezekiel

2. Which Jamaican sang *The Train is Coming* for the sound track of the movie *Money Train*?
   Ans. Shaggy

3. True or false? Sulphur is enantiotrophic.
   Ans. True

4. Give a word ending with the letters "ate" which means to cut off a part of a person's body which is infected.
   Ans. Amputate

5. With which French leader did Pope Pius VII execute the Concordat of 1801?
   Ans. Napoleon

6. Which was the first labour of Hercules?
   Ans. Killing the Nemean lion

7. What medical term denotes a lack of symmetry in the shape of the cornea?
   Ans. Astigmatism

8. What is the capital of Chechnya?
   Ans. Grozny

9. Which of the following does not have a trigonal planar shape: NO_3^-, CO_3^{2-} or NH_3?
   Ans. NH_3

10. He qualified as a surgeon at St. Thomas' Hospital in London, and drew material from this for his novel *Of Human Bondage*. Name him.
    Ans. Somerset Maugham

11. Who composed the music for the opera *The Mikado*?
    Ans. Arthur Sullivan

12. Whose law in physics states the relationship between the extension of a spiral spring and the load on the spring?
    Ans. Hooke's Law

13. By what other name is the Islamic Resistance Movement known in the Middle East?
    Ans. Hamas

14. Carbaritta Isle acts as a natural breakwater for which harbour in Jamaica?
    Ans. Port Maria

15. What is the next prime number after 61?
    Ans. 67

16. A lens has focal distance of 100 mm. What is its power in dioptres?
    Ans. 10 D

17. What is the nationality of the footballer George Weah?
    Ans. Liberian

18. Who invented the stethoscope?
    Ans. Laennec

19. The production of which agricultural item is affected by the American fowl brood disease?
    Ans. Honey

20. Which English king was known as the Wisest Fool in Christendom?
    Ans. King James I

21. What is the SI unit of specific heat?
    Ans. Joules/kg/kelvin

22. In *The Sound of Music*, what was the name of the family which employed Maria?
    Ans. The Von Trapp family

23. What is the value of $(0.02)^2$?
    Ans. 0.0004

24. In which Caribbean colony did Lord Harris serve during the mid-nineteenth century?
    Ans. Trinidad

25. Give the meaning of the Spanish verb *crecer*.
    Ans. To increase

26. Which Jamaican entertainer had the hit song *Till I Am Laid to Rest*?
    Ans. Buju Banton

27. Pyrolusite is an ore of which metal?
    Ans. Manganese

28. Which West Indian wrote the essays in the book *The Overcrowded Barracoon*?
    Ans. V.S. Naipaul

29. What medical condition is caused by a lack of Vitamin D?
    Ans. Ricketts

30. Who first devised the steam hammer: James Watt, James Nasmyth or George Stephenson?
    Ans. James Nasmyth

31. Give the meaning of the abbreviation ACP in international affairs.
    Ans. African, Caribbean and Pacific

32. What is 0.49 divided by 0.7?
    Ans. 0.7

33. Spell the word ENNUI.

34. In which African country is the city of Mombasa located: Tanzania, Kenya or Ghana?
    Ans. Kenya

35. Name the Shakespearean play which was put on at the opening of the Globe Theatre.
    Ans. *Henry V*

36. Which French artist was imprisoned for his caricatures depicting King Louis Philippe as having a pear-shaped head?
    Ans. Daumier

37. State the chemical formula for Glauber's salt.
    Ans. $Na_2SO_4.10H_2O$

38. Which political party in Trinidad and Tobago is abbreviated as the PNM?
    Ans. People's National Movement

39. The mean of two numbers is 95. If one number is 24, what is the other?
    Ans. 166

40. Which vitamin, found in green vegetables, is also formed by bacteria in the intestines?
    Ans. Vitamin K

III. Signal Section

Bible Knowledge

1. What name in the Bible is shared by a Jewish high priest before whom Paul was tried, a Christian of Damascus who received Paul, and a Christian in Jerusalem who lost his life for lying?
    Ans. Ananias

Mathematics

2. The angles of a triangle are in the ratio of 5:4:1. What is the size of the largest angle?
    Ans. 90 degrees

Foreign Languages

3. In Spanish, which animal is referred to as *el caballo*?
    Ans. Horse

Physics

4. The discovery of which principle in physics provoked the cry of "Eureka!"?
    Ans. Archimedes Principle

Geography

5. In which American State is the geographical centre of North America located: is it North Dakota, South Dakota or Nevada?
    Ans. North Dakota

Literature

6. Which novelist won the Pulitzer Prize in 1953 and the Nobel Prize for Literature in 1954?
    Ans. Ernest Hemingway

History

7. Jamaica was captured by the English in 1655, but in what year did England and Spain first agree by treaty that Jamaica should remain under English control?
    Ans. 1670 (Treaty of Madrid)

English Language

8. Form a noun from the word "obese".
    Ans. Obesity

Chemistry

9. Which of the following is the strongest reducing agent: fluorine, lithium or zinc?
    Ans. Lithium

Sports

10. Which West Indian pace bowler ended with match figures of 10 for 92 in the 1988 Test match between the West Indies and England at Lord's?
    Ans. Malcolm Marshall

General Knowledge

11. What is the meaning of the abbreviation OECS in international affairs?
    Ans. Organization of Eastern Caribbean States

Foreign Languages

12. Give the meaning of the Spanish expression *hecho un mar de lagrimas*?
    Ans. In a flood of tears

Physics

13. A uniform wire, fixed at its upper end, hangs vertically and supports a weight at its lower end. If its radius is r and its length is L, is the extension inversely proportional to r or directly proportional to L?

    Ans. Directly proportional to L

Biology

14. Who first explained heredity by showing that traits are passed in predictable patterns?

    Ans. Gregor Mendel

Jamaican Heritage

15. In which Jamaican parish is the Maroon town of Accompong located?

    Ans. St. Elizabeth

Theatre and Cinema

16. Which actor starred in the 1925 movie *The Gold Rush*: Charlie Chaplin, Stewart Granger or John Wayne?

    Ans. Charlie Chaplain

Literature

17. Which British philosopher, mathematician and pacifist received the 1950 Nobel Prize for Literature for his book *Marriage and Morals*?

    Ans. Bertrand Russell

Mathematics

18. What is the value of $\frac{2}{25}$ as a decimal?

    Ans. 0.08

Bible Knowledge

19. Which Old Testament character did God promise "Your descendants will be as many as the stars in the sky"?

    Ans. Abraham

General Knowledge

20. How many keys are there on a standard piano?

    Ans. 88

Music

21. In which opera by Verdi would you find the main characters Violetta and Alfredo?

    Ans. *La Traviata*

Local and International Affairs

22. Which country became the 14th member of the Caribbean Community in January 1996?

    Ans. Suriname

Geography

23. What name is given to the treeless, permanently frozen northern regions of the world: tundra, steppes or pampas?

    Ans. Tundra

Mathematics

24. Given that $^-2x - 6 = {}^-7$, what is the value of x^2?

    Ans. $\frac{1}{4}$

English Language

25. State the figurative expression taken from mathematics which means to change suddenly to a different course of thought or action.

    Ans. To go off at a tangent

Literature

26. Which West Indian wrote the book *The Pleasures of Exile*?

    Ans. George Lamming

Foreign Languages

27. Which French verb means both "to have lunch" and "to have breakfast"?
    Ans. *Dejeuner*

Physics

28. Name the apparatus in physics in which charged particles leave miniature vapour trails that reveal their paths.
    Ans. Wilson Cloud Chamber

History

29. At the time of British slave emancipation in the Caribbean, which of the Leeward Islands opted not to introduce the Apprenticeship System?
    Ans. Antigua

Biology

30. Mary is reading a book. She then looks out of a window to focus on a tree. Does the lens in her eye become thinner, fatter or shorter?
    Ans. Thinner

Sports

31. With which sport do you associate the name Larry Gomes in the Caribbean?
    Ans. Cricket

General Knowledge

32. What is the more popular name for the West Indian manatee?
    Ans. The Sea Cow

Chemistry

33. Does the coagulating effect of an ion depend on the size, magnitude of charge, or speed of the ion?
    Ans. The magnitude of the ion

Art

34. Which European sculpted *The Age of Bronze* which he put on display in 1977?
    Ans. Rodin

Mythology

35. Name the runner who is said to have run with the news of the victory of the Athenians at Marathon.
    Ans. Pheidippides

Sports

36. Which two teams contest for the Sir Frank Worrell Trophy in Test cricket?
    Ans. The West Indies and Australia

Geography

37. In which Caribbean island would you find the sulphur springs town of Soufriere?
    Ans. St. Lucia

General Knowledge

38. Give one word for the study of rocks.
    Ans. Petrology

Literature

39. In which Shakespearean play does the character Launcelot Gobbo appear?
    Ans. *The Merchant of Venice*

Physics

40. True or false? Both sound and light can be refracted.
    Ans. True

Quiz No. 8

I. Alternate Section

English Language

1. Give a word ending with the letters "ate" which means to "disinfect or purify with fumes".
   Ans. Fumigate

2. Give a word ending with the letters "ate" which means to "punish with blows or words, to chastise".
   Ans. Castigate

Sports

3. In the history of Test cricket, which batsman has the third highest score for a single innings?
   Ans. Len Hutton

4. In the history of Test cricket, Sanath Jayasuriya has the fourth highest score for a single innings. How much is it?
   Ans. 340

Chemistry

5. What is the atomic number of aluminium?
   Ans. 13

6. What is the atomic number of carbon?
   Ans. 6

Literature

7. In Shakespeare's *The Tempest*, who was the lovely and innocent daughter of Prospero?
   Ans. Miranda

8. In Shakespeare's *Macbeth* who was the Thane of Fife?
   Ans. Macduff

Physics

9. Which of the following terms denotes the emission of light at low temperatures: luminosity, luminescence or light energy?
   Ans. Luminescence

10. Which of the following terms denotes the production of charged ions from electrically neutral atoms or molecular fragments: ionization, interference or phosphorescence?
    Ans. Ionization

General Knowledge

11. Who received the Norman Manley Award for Excellence in 1998, for his contribution to science in Jamaica?
    Ans. Gerald Lalor

12. Name the first Director General of the Office of Utilities Regulation in Jamaica.
    Ans. Winston Hay

Biology

13. True or false? A mutation is a natural spontaneous change in the structure of RNA in chromosomes.
    Ans. False (DNA)

14. True or false? Mutations cannot be induced in organisms by exposure to excessive radiation.
    Ans. False

Music

15. What term in music denotes both the voice of boys before puberty and the highest female voice?
    Ans. Soprano

16. What term in music denotes the playing of strings by plucking them?
    Ans. Pizzicato

Jamaican Heritage

17. Two adjoining bays in Jamaica are so-called because cattle used to be slaughtered and cured nearby. Cow Bay is one, which is the other?
    Ans. Bull Bay

18. In which parish would you find Bustamante Bridge?
    Ans. St. Thomas

Theatre and Cinema

19. Which Jamaican actress had a significant role in both *Trapper John, M.D.* and *Star Trek — The Next Generation*?
    Ans. Madge Sinclair

20. Which Jamaican was posthumously awarded the Doctor Bird Award for his work as producer and director of television programmes such as *Perspective*, *Lime Tree Lane* and *Heritage*?
    Ans. Donat "Don" Bucknor

Mathematics

21. What is 198 rounded off to one significant figure?
    Ans. 200

22. What is 5.0465 to 2 decimal places?
    Ans. 5.05

History

23. In 1859, which American abolitionist led a group of 20 men in a raid on Harper's Ferry, West Virginia?
    Ans. John Brown

24. In 1916, who opened the first birth control clinic?
    Ans. Margaret Sanger

Religious Knowledge

25. What name is given to the Christian sacrament that celebrates the Lord's Supper?
    Ans. The Eucharist

26. What term denotes the belief that the bread and wine used in the Eucharist are changed into the body and blood of Christ?
    Ans. Transubstantiation

Biology

27. In which part of the body would you find the cervical vertebrae?
    Ans. Neck

28. Give the biological name for the shoulder blade.
    Ans. Scapula

Sports

29. Which Jamaican won two bronze medals at the 1960 Olympic Games, one for the 800 metres and the other for the 4x400 metres relay?
    Ans. George Kerr

30. How many Olympic medals has Donald Quarrie won?
    Ans. 4

Physics

31. A body starting at rest moves to a velocity of 10 metres per second in 2.5 seconds. What is the acceleration of the body?
    Ans. 4 metres per second squared

32. A body moving initially with a velocity of 27 metres per second comes to rest after 6 seconds. What is the deceleration of the body?
    Ans. 4.5 metres per second squared

Theatre and Cinema

33. Who wrote the play *Champagne and Sky Juice*?
    Ans. Basil Dawkins

34. Name the male star of the movie *Les Miserables*.
    Ans. Liam Neeson

English Language

35. Give one word which means both "the cost of a journey" and "food provided".
    Ans. Fare

36. Give one word which means both "to abstain from food" and "firmly fixed".
    Ans. Fast

General Knowledge

37. With which field of activity in Jamaica do you associate Cecil Baugh?
    Ans. Pottery

38. Who sculpted the statue of National Hero Paul Bogle?
    Ans. Edna Manley

Geography

39. What term denotes the theory which considers the crust of the earth to be made of huge rigid blocks called plates?
    Ans. Tectonic theory

40. According to the tectonic theory, how many major plates are there?
    Ans. 7

II. The Speed Section

Speed Questions for Team A

1. Is time a vector or a scalar quantity?
   Ans. Scalar

2. The main thought of which religion is set out in a series of writings known as the Upanishads: Buddhism or Hinduism?
   Ans. Hinduism

3. What is 0.875 expressed as a fraction in its lowest terms?
   Ans. $\frac{7}{8}$

4. Which famous Jamaican singer has an album entitled *Higher and Higher*?
   Ans. Jimmy Cliff

5. Which country will host the World Cup for football in 2006?
   Ans. Germany

6. Spell the word FLUORESCENT.

7. What was the title traditionally given to rulers of the Buganda people of Africa?
   Ans. Kabaka

8. In which city were the main Nazi leaders subject to trial for war crimes following World War II?
   Ans. Nuremberg, Germany

9. Give the meaning of the French infinitive *chercher*.
   Ans. To look for

10. Which African-American wrote the book *I Know Why the Caged Bird Sings*?
    Ans. Maya Angelou

11. Which element has atomic mass 19?
    Ans. Fluorine

12. Who played the lead male and female roles in the 1952 classic *Singin' in the Rain*?
    Ans. Gene Kelly and Debbie Reynolds

13. In which parish of Jamaica is Manchioneal located?
    Ans. Portland

14. Give the biological name for the shinbone.
    Ans. Tibia

15. What is the SI unit of radiant flux?
    Ans. The watt

16. Who wrote the book *Edna Manley: Sculptures* in 1998?
    Ans. David Boxer, curator of the National Gallery

17. What is the capital of Grenada?
    Ans. St. George's

18. Which term denotes the traditional form of praise to God which includes the phrase "Glory be to God"?
    Ans. Doxology

19. What is the value of 764,000 in standard form?
    Ans. 7.64×10^5

20. Which movie about dockside workers who challenge corrupt labour leaders won the Academy Award for Best Picture for 1954?
    Ans. *On the Waterfront*

21. Name the two Australian batsmen who share the highest score for their country in Test Cricket.
    Ans. Don Bradman and Mark Taylor

22. In what century did Giuseppe Garibaldi lead the Red-shirts: 18th or 19th?
    Ans. 19th

23. With which trade union in Jamaica do you associate the name James Francis?
    Ans. Union of Jamaica (the UUJ)

24. Which musical term is derived from Latin meaning "in church music style"?
    Ans. *A cappella*

25. Spell the word ANONYMOUS.

26. Which phylum in biology consists of microscopic unicellular animals?
    Ans. Protozoa

27. Who did the series of engravings called *Marriage a la Mode*?
    Ans. William Hogarth

28. In what year was Newcastle established?
    Ans. 1941

29. Who was the second husband of Jacqueline Kennedy?
    Ans. Aristotle Onassis

30. In which country is there a city named Quezon City?
    Ans. The Philippines

31. Where in the body would you find the tarsals?
    Ans. The ankle

32. What term denotes an electrical machine for converting alternating current voltage to higher or lower voltage?
    Ans. Transformer

33. What is 25% of 10% of 44?
    Ans. 1.1

34. By what name was the cricketer O'Neil Gordon Smith more popularly known?
    Ans. Collie Smith

35. "Wait a minute! Wait a minute! Yu ain't heard nothin' yet!" Whose words were these in 1927?
    Ans. Al Jolson, in *The Jazz Singer*, the first talking movie

36. Which Latin phrase denotes the list of characters in a play?
    Ans. *Dramatis personae*

37. Who sculpted the statue of Noel Nethersole which stands outside the Bank of Jamaica?
    Ans. Kay Sullivan

38. At the end of the decade of the 1990s, which agricultural product was marketed overseas under the commercial name "Jamaica Blue"?
    Ans. Coffee

39. In which country would you find the headquarters of the Leeward Islands Air Transport (LIAT)?
    Ans. Antigua

40. What name was given to the line of defensive fortifications built along France's north-eastern frontier from Switzerland to Luxembourg, completed in 1936.
    Ans. Maginot Line

Speed Questions for Team B

1. Is distance a scalar or a vector quantity?
   Ans. Scalar

2. Which term is used in the Hindu religion to denote action: karma or samsara?
   Ans. Karma

3. What is 0.45 expressed as a fraction in its lowest terms?
   Ans. $\frac{9}{20}$

4. Which honorary degree has been conferred upon Jimmy Cliff by the University of the West Indies?
   Ans. Doctor of Letters

5. Name the coach of the Brazilian football team which won the World Cup in 2002.
   Ans. Phil Scolari

6. Spell the word OMINOUS.

7. What was the title traditionally given to Turkish governors and to the ruler of Tunisia?
   Ans. Bey

8. In what year did the Cuban Missile Crisis take place?
   Ans. 1962

9. Give the meaning of the French infinitive *regarder*.
   Ans. To look at

10. Which African-American wrote the book, *Beloved*?
    Ans. Toni Morrison

11. Which element has atomic mass 14?
    Ans. Nitrogen

12. Which two men had the lead roles in the 1993 movie classic *Schindler's List*?
    Ans. Liam Neeson and Ben Kingsley

13. Which Jamaican wrote the screenplay for the presentation *Fight Against Slavery*?
    Ans. Evan Jones

14. Off the coast of which Jamaican port is Navy Island located?
    Ans. Port Antonio

15. What is the SI unit of potential difference?
    Ans. The volt

16. Where on the body would you find the phalanges?
    Ans. Toes, fingers

17. Name the Portuguese writer who won the Nobel Prize for Literature in 1998.
    Ans. José Saramago

18. What is the capital of Pakistan?
    Ans. Islamabad

19. The name of this religious group literally means "spirit fighters" in Russian, and the group shows some likeness in doctrine to the Quakers. Name the group.
    Ans. Doukhobors

20. What is the value of 80 divided by 0.125?
    Ans. 640

21. Who was the male star of the movie *On the Waterfront*?
    Ans. Marlon Brando

22. Give the meaning of the musical term *accelerando*?
    Ans. Becoming gradually faster

23. In what century was Alexander Hamilton killed in a duel: 18th or 19th?
    Ans. 19th

24. What is the score shared by Don Bradman and Mark Taylor as the highest by Australian batsmen?
    Ans. 334

25. Which Spanish surrealist painted the murals of the UNESCO buildings in Paris?
    Ans. Joan Miro

26. With which trade union in Jamaica do you associate the name Carlyle Dunkley?
    Ans. National Workers Union

27. Spell the word NUANCE.

27. Which phylum in biology consists of porous animals often occurring in colonies, for example sponges?
    Ans. Porifera

28. In what year did the Carib Theatre fire take place?
    Ans. 1996

29. What was Jacqueline Kennedy's maiden name?
    Ans. Jacqueline Bouvier

30. In which country is there a city named Oporto?
    Ans. Portugal

31. Which branch of mechanics deals with the study of fluids at rest?
    Ans. Hydrostatics

32. Where in the body would you find the patella?
    Ans. The knee cap

33. What is $12\frac{1}{2}\%$ of 50% of 240?
    Ans. 15

34. Only three cricketers have scored a century and taken 5 wickets in an innings of the same Test match. Name two of them.
    Ans. Garfield Sobers, Collie Smith, Denis Atkinson

35. Identify the first film made in the James Bond series.
    Ans. *Dr No*

36. What is the meaning of the Latin phrase *de mortuis nil nisi bonum*?
    Ans. Nothing but good should be spoken of the dead.

37. Who sculpted the statue of Sir Alexander Bustamante which stands at South Parade in Kingston?
    Ans. Alvin Marriot

38. Which Jamaican agency is abbreviated as the SRC?
    Ans. The Scientific Research Council

39. In which country would you find the headquarters of the BWIA Airways?
    Ans. Trinidad and Tobago

40. What name was given to the boundary line between Pennsylvania and Maryland, laid out in the 18th century, which represented the division between northern states and the slave-owning states of the South?
    Ans. Mason-Dixon Line

III. The Signal Section

Bible Knowledge

1. Which biblical character said, "My father, my father, the horsemen of Israel and the chariots thereof."?
   Ans. Elisha

Geography

2. Which is the highest mountain peak in Greece?
   Ans. Mount Olympus

Biology

3. Which phylum in biology consists of tentacle-bearing animals with stinging cells?
   Ans. Coelenterata

General Knowledge

4. What is the meaning of the acronym USAID?
   Ans. United States Agency for International Development

Jamaican Heritage

5. Name the Jamaican custom similar to a "wake" in other countries.
   Ans. Nine Night

Mathematics

6. If 5 to the power of minus x is equal to 625, what is the value of x?
   Ans. $^-4$

Geography

7. In which parish of Jamaica is the Martha Brae River?
   Ans. Trelawny

History

8. In what year did French forces under Napoleon retreat from Moscow?
   Ans. 1812

Theatre and Cinema

9. Identify the movie, based on a novel by Charles Webb, in which a 20 year old student, Ben, enters into a relationship with the much older Mrs. Robinson?
   Ans. *The Graduate*

Biology

10. Name the two main places in the body where lymphocytes are formed.
    Ans. Spleen and lymph nodes

General Knowledge

11. What is the unit of currency in Thailand?
    Ans. The Baht

Art

12. Which Dutch artist painted *The Laughing Cavalier*?
    Ans. Frans Hals

Chemistry

13. What term denotes the phenomenon in which two or more compounds exist with the same chemical formula but with different structures?
    Ans. Isomerism

History

14. In what year was the Spanish House of Trade established?
    Ans. 1503

General Knowledge

15. Which Jamaican organization has its headquarters at Jacisera Park?
    Ans. Jamaica Civil Service Association

English Language

16. If something is done in a didactic manner, what does this mean?
    Ans. It is meant to instruct; having the manner of a teacher

Jamaican Heritage

17. Which people introduced the plantain to Jamaica?
    Ans. The Spanish

Mathematics

18. Express 580 g as a percentage of 2 kg.
    Ans. 29%

General Knowledge

19. Name the religious group which controlled the government of Afghanistan in the period immediately preceding the attacks on the World Trade Centre on September 11, 2001.
    Ans. The Taliban

Biology

20. To which phylum do segmented worms belong?
    Ans. Annelida

Geography

21. In which continent is there a city named Nice?
    Ans. Europe

Music

22. In which 1939 movie did Judy Garland sing *Over the Rainbow* which won the Academy Award for Best Song?
    Ans. *The Wizard of Oz*

Sports

23. How many Olympic medals did Arthur Wint win?
    Ans. 4

Chemistry

24. What is the atomic number of sodium?
    Ans. 11

General Knowledge

25. If you were born between May 21 and June 21, what would be your astrological sign?
    Ans. Gemini

English Language

26. Spell the word PSYCHE.

Music

27. In 1997, which Jamaican singer celebrated 30 years in music with a concert billed *Life is Just for Living*?
    Ans. Ernie Smith

Theatre and Cinema

28. Name the male star of the movie *Casablanca*.
    Ans. Humphrey Bogart

Jamaican Heritage

29. In what year was Sam Sharpe born?
    Ans. 1801

Mathematics

30. What is the value of the square root of 512 expressed as a surd in its lowest terms?
    Ans. 16 root 2

Art

31. Which artist painted the frescoes for the Sistine Chapel?
    Ans. Michelangelo

Physics

32. True or false? Momentum is a scalar quantity.
    Ans. False

Local and International Affairs

33. What is the meaning of the abbreviation UNFPA?
    Ans. United Nations Population Fund

Geography

34. In which parish of Jamaica is Accompong Town located?
    Ans. St. Elizabeth

Theatre and Cinema

35. Who produced and directed the movie *The Harder They Come*?
    Ans. Perry Henzell

History

36. The Battle of Edgehill was the first battle in which war?
    Ans. The English Civil War

General Knowledge

37. How many satellites are known to be in the orbit of the planet Mercury?
    Ans. None

Literature

38. What is an eclogue?
    Ans. A short poem, particularly a pastoral dialogue between shepherds

Jamaican Heritage

39. With which field of activity in Jamaica do you associate the name Franklyn St. Juste?
    Ans. Cinematography

Biology

40. What type of joint is there at the wrist?
    Ans. Gliding

Quiz No. 9

I. The Alternate Section

Jamaican Heritage

1. Name the two Jamaican parishes where towns called Aboukir may be found.
   Ans. St. Ann and Trelawny

2. Name the two Jamaican parishes where towns called Lilliput may be found.
   Ans. St. Elizabeth and St. James

Mathematics

3. What is the value of $(\frac{1}{3})^{-5}$
   Ans. 243

4. What is the value of $4^{-\frac{5}{2}}$
   Ans. $\frac{1}{32}$

History

5. What term denoted the signed agreements or documents which related to each of the Indian and Chinese immigrants who came to the West Indies mainly in the 19th and early 20th centuries?
   Ans. Indentures

6. Which British West Indian colony had no apprenticeship system following the abolition of slavery in the 19th century?
   Ans. Antigua

Biology

7. Which two hormones are responsible for the development of the follicle and ovum as well as for ovulation in women?
   Ans. Oestrogen and the Follicle Stimulating Hormone

8. Which hormone ensures that the lining of the uterus is retained and does not break down in women?
   Ans. Progesterone

Sports

9. Three West Indians have scored a century in their first match against Australia in Test cricket. Name two.
   Ans. Maurice Foster, Clive Lloyd, Collie Smith

10. Identify the two sports most associated with the Jamaican Maurice Foster.
    Ans. Cricket and table tennis

English Language

11. Spell the homonym of "b-e-a-c-h".
    Ans. Beech

12. Spell the homonym of "b-o-l-d-e-r".
    Ans. Boulder

General Knowledge

13. What name is given to the meeting of Roman Catholic Cardinals to elect a new pope?

    Ans. Conclave

14. Which group of people are sometimes referred to as the "princes" of the Roman Catholic Church?

    Ans. Cardinals

Geography

15. What is the highest point in Haiti?

    Ans. Pico Duarte

16. In which Caribbean country would you find the Sierra Maestra?

    Ans. Cuba

Physics

17. True or false? Whenever a ray travels from a medium to a less dense medium, refraction takes place away from the normal.

    Ans. True

18. True or false? The critical angle is only possible for light travelling from a dense to a less dense medium.

    Ans. True

Foreign Languages

19. What is the meaning of the Spanish command *Diganles*?

    Ans. Tell them.

20. What is the meaning of the Spanish command *Comprenlo*?

    Ans. Buy it.

Literature

21. Which historical event forms the basis of the novel *New Day* by Vic Reid?

    Ans. The Morant Bay Rebellion

22. Which historical event forms the background to the novel *The Leopard* by Vic Reid?

    Ans. The Mau Mau Rebellion in Kenya

Art

23. Which European artist painted *Cornfield with Flight of Birds*?

    Ans. Van Gogh

24. Which European artist painted *The Hireling Shepherd*?

    Ans. Holman Hunt

Chemistry

25. What term denotes the heat evolved when 1 mole of water is formed during a reaction between an acid and a base?

    Ans. Heat of neutralisation

26. What term denotes the heat evolved when 1 mole of a substance is completely burned in oxygen?

    Ans. Heat of combustion

Local and International Affairs

27. Who was the chairman of the committee set up to identify the location of the International Seabed Authority in Jamaica.

    Ans. Lloyd Barnett

28. Who was the first Executive Director of the Fair Trading Commission in Jamaica?

    Ans. Geraldine Foster

Mathematics

29. What is the mathematical formula for the volume of a cylinder?

    Ans. Pi r squared h (where r is the base radius and h is the height)

30. What is the mathematical formula for the volume of a cone?

   Ans. One third pi r squared h (where r is the base radius and h is the height)

Foreign Languages

31. What is the opposite, in French, of the word *faible*?

   Ans. *Fort*

32. What is the opposite, in French, of the word *sur*?

   Ans. *Sous*

Mythology

33. Who was the Roman equivalent to the Greek god of war, Ares?

   Ans. Mars

34. Who was the Roman equivalent to the Greek god of wine, Dionysius?

   Ans. Bacchus

History

35. Who was the first Prime Minister of Great Britain?

   Ans. Sir Robert Walpole

36. Who was Prime Minister of Great Britain from 1940 to 1945 and from 1951 to 1955?

   Ans. Sir Winston Churchill

English Language

37. What is the past participle of the verb "swell"?

   Ans. Swollen

38. What is the past participle of the verb "tear"?

   Ans. Torn

Physics

39. The position of a particle moving along the x-axis is given by $x = 2 + 3t + 4t^3$. What is its velocity after 2 seconds?

   Ans. 51 m/s

40. The position of a particle moving along the x-axis is given by $x = 4 - 27t + t^3$. At what time is its velocity zero?

   Ans. 3 m/s

I. The Speed Section

Speed Questions for Team A

1. Give the meaning of the abbreviation UHWI in Jamaica.
   Ans. University Hospital of the West Indies

2. Spell the word PRESCRIPTION.

3. Which was the longest and bloodiest battle of World War I?
   Ans. The Battle of Verdun

4. True or false? In a solar eclipse, the sun comes between the earth and the moon.
   Ans. False

5. In which town is Nanny of the Maroons buried?
   Ans. Moore Town

6. In geography, what is a solfatara?
   Ans. A volcanic vent that emits hot gases and vapours

7. Change all singulars into plurals: "The deer was grazing on the hillside".
   Ans. The deer were grazing on the hillsides.

8. Factorise $x^2 + 6x + 9$.
   Ans. $(x + 3)(x + 3)$

9. Give the Spanish word for "cheap".
   Ans. *Barato*

10. In biology, what is dysmenorrhoea?
    Ans. Muscular cramps and backache women sometimes experience during the period of menstrual flow

11. Who was the Roman Queen of the gods?
    Ans. Juno

12. Give the meaning of the French *le chien*.
    Ans. The dog

13. What is the past participle of the verb "hit"?
    Ans. Hit

14. What is the other name for German measles?
    Ans. Rubella

15. Give the meaning of the abbreviation PAC in South Africa.
    Ans. Pan Africanist Congress

16. In which two Caribbean countries would you find mountain ranges known as the Cordillera Central?
    Ans. Haiti and Puerto Rico

17. In computer terminology, what is meant by the abbreviation LSI?
    Ans. Large Scale Integration

18. What is the next number in the series: 9, 16, 36, 81?
    Ans. 169

19. What is the nationality of the tennis player Jonas Bjorkman?
    Ans. Swedish

20. Who painted *Ann of Cleves*?
    Ans. Hans Holbein (the Younger)

21. Form a noun from the adjective "cynical".
    Ans. Cynicism

22. Which gland in the body controls blood calcium levels?
    Ans. Thyroid

23. Which Jamaican is the subject of the book *Anthology of a Hero*?
    Ans. Bustamante

24. If p * q = 2p + q, what is the value of $\frac{1}{2}$ * 3?
    Ans. 5

25. Give the name of the trophy competed for in Sharjah by Test cricketers.
    Ans. Champions Trophy

26. What is the capital of Turkmenstan?
    Ans. Ashkhabad

27. Which European leader was known as *El caudillo*?
    Ans. General Franco

28. What is the meaning of the Spanish word *bonito*?
    Ans. Pretty

29. In which parish is Vernamfield Racing Track located?
    Ans. Clarendon

30. In what year was the University of Technology established as the College of Arts, Science and Technology?
    Ans. 1958

31. Which Jamaican entertainer is popularly known as "Grub"?
    Ans. Astley Cooper

32. Which type of mango in Jamaica shares its name with a famous English admiral?
    Ans. Nelson

33. Give the meaning of the abbreviation WPM in Jamaica?
    Ans. Western Parks and Markets

34. Who painted *L'Escargot*?
    Ans. Henri Matisse

35. Who was the muse of lyrical poetry and music in Greek mythology?
    Ans. Euterpe

36. True or false? A body is said to be at a positive potential when electrons flow up into it from the sun.
    Ans. False

37. In which parish of Jamaica would you find Comfort Castle?
    Ans. Portland

38. With which sport do you most associate the name Jack Villeneuve?
    Ans. Motor racing

39. Who was Prime Minister of Great Britain from 1976 to 1979?
    Ans. Jim Callaghan

40. Explain the figurative expression "to have the game in one's hand".
    Ans. To be certain of winning

Speed Questions for Team B

1. Give the meaning of the abbreviation NDFJ in Jamaica.
   Ans. National Development Foundation of Jamaica

2. Spell the word PRACTITIONER.

3. In what year did the Battle of Verdun take place?
   Ans. 1916

4. True or false? In a lunar eclipse the moon comes between the sun and the earth.
   Ans. False

5. What name is given to Nanny's grave?
   Ans. Bump Grave

6. Which country is richer in hot springs and solfataras than any other?
   Ans. Iceland

7. Change all singulars into plurals: "The man ate a large sheep."
   Ans. The men ate some large sheep.

8. Factorise $x^2 - 2x + 1$.
   Ans. $(x - 1)(x - 1)$

9. Give the Spanish for "the armchair".
   Ans. *El sillon*

10. In biology, what term denotes the absence of the monthly menstrual flow among women?
    Ans. Amenorrhoea

11. Who was the Roman god of the underworld?
    Ans. Pluto

12. Give the meaning of the French *donc*.
    Ans. So; therefore

13. What is the past participle of the verb "bring"?
    Ans. Brought

14. Name the structure which links the embryo to the placenta in humans.
    Ans. The umbilical cord (or umbilicus)

15. Give the meaning of the abbreviation ANC in South Africa.
    Ans. African National Congress

16. In which Caribbean country would you find the Northern Range?
    Ans. Trinidad

17. In computer terminology, what is meant by the abbreviation RAM?
    Ans. Random Access Memory

18. What is the next number in the series: 3, 11, 20, 30?
    Ans. 41

19. What is the nationality of the tennis player Gusavo Kuerten?
    Ans. Brazilian

20. Who painted many portraits of Charles I?
    Ans. Anthony van Dyck

21. Form a noun from the adjective "cyclical".
    Ans. Cycle

22. Which glands in the body produces hydrocortisone, as well as the fight or flight hormone?
   Ans. Adrenal glands

23. Which Jamaican wrote the book *Anthology of a Hero* about one of the country's national heroes?
   Ans. B. St. J. Hamilton

24. If p * q = 4p – q, what is the value of $1\frac{1}{2} * 2$?
   Ans. 4

25. In which country is Sharjah is located?
   Ans. United Arab Emirates

26. What is the capital of Uzbekistan?
   Ans. Tashkent

27. Which European leader was known as *Il duce*?
   Ans. Mussolini

28. What is the meaning of the Spanish verb *enviar*?
   Ans. To send

29. In which parish of Jamaica is the Dover Raceway located?
   Ans. St. Ann

30. In what year was the University of the West Indies established?
   Ans. 1948

31. Which Jamaican entertainer is popularly known as "Billy Mystic"?
   Ans. Anthony Wilmot

32. Which type of mango in Jamaica takes its name largely from its place of origin?
   Ans. East Indian

33. Give the meaning of the acronym NASA?
   Ans. National Aeronautics and Space Administration

34. Who painted *Christ in the Hands of Martha*?
   Ans. Jan Vermeer

35. Who was the muse of tragedy in Greek mythology?
   Ans. Melpomene

36. True or false? A body is said to be at a negative potential when electrons flow from it to the earth.
   Ans. True

37. In which parish of Jamaica would you find Macca Tree?
   Ans. St. Catherine

38. What is the nationality of Jack Villeneuve?
   Ans. Canadian

39. Who was Prime Minister of Great Britain from 1964 to 1970, and from 1974 to 1976?
   Ans. Harold Wilson

40. Explain the figurative expression "to run the gauntlet".
   Ans. To receive blows from all sides; to be criticised on all quarters

III. The Signal Section

Bible Knowledge

1. Which biblical character said: "I am a Jew, from Tarsus in Cilicia, a citizen of no ordinary city."?
   Ans. Paul

Biology

2. In biology, what term denotes the soft hair covering the body of the human foetus?
   Ans. Lanugo

Mathematics

3. What is the smallest value of x if cos 2x = 0.5?
   Ans. 30 degrees

Jamaican Heritage

4. Novelist, poet, painter, playwright and political activist, he was a volunteer constable in Jamaica in 1938, when, on his way to quell waterfront riots, he decided to support the rioters instead. Name him.
   Ans. Roger Mais

Sports

5. Name any two of the West Indian bowlers who have taken over 300 wickets in Test cricket.
   Ans. Lance Gibbs, Malcolm Marshall, Courtney Walsh, Courtley Ambrose

History

6. Which American President developed the Good Neighbour policy?
   Ans. F.D. Roosevelt

Physics

7. True or false? Displacement is a scalar quantity.
   Ans. False

Music

8. Which Jamaican singer put out the album *Midnight Lover* in 1997?
   Ans. Shaggy

Foreign Languages

9. Give the meaning of the Spanish *no les diga*.
   Ans. Do not tell them.

Art

10. Who painted *The Sistine Madonna*?
    Ans. Raphael

Proverbs and Idioms

11. Explain the Jamaican proverb "Anancy say, two chubble betta dan wan."
    Ans. It is sometimes easier to handle several problems when they come at the same time, rather than to handle them singly.

English Language

12. Give a four-letter word beginning with "b" which means to talk or tell foolishly or indiscreetly.
    Ans. Blab

Chemistry

13. Which chemist adapted the Haber process for industrial production?
    Ans. Bosch

Mathematics

14. Increase $400 by 20%.
    Ans. $480

General Knowledge

15. In 1965, which West Indian wrote a long essay on the collapse of the West Indies Federation entitled *The Agony of the Eight*?
    Ans. Arthur Lewis

Jamaican Heritage

16. By what more popular name do we know the Jamaica People's Museum of Craft and Technology, located in Spanish Town Square?
    Ans. The Folk Museum

Biology

17. Which gland in the body produces growth hormones, prolactin and stimulates the sexual glands?
    Ans. Pituitary

Local and International Affairs

18. In which Caribbean country is there a prominent sect known as the Jamaat Al Muslimeen?
    Ans. Trinidad and Tobago

Physics

19. How much heat is required to take ice of mass 2 kg at ⁻10 degree centigrade to ice at 0 degrees centigrade if the specific heat capacity of ice is 2,200 J/kg K?
    Ans. 44,000 J

Theatre and Cinema

20. Who played the role of "Junior", a character who temporarily loses his mind, in the movie *Dance Hall Queen*?
    Ans. Mark Danvers

Foreign Languages

21. Give the meaning of the Latin *in camera*.
    Ans. In secret

General Knowledge

22. "What hath God wrought!" was the first message sent, in 1844, by which mechanism?
    Ans. The wireless telegraph (Morse)

Bible Knowledge

23. Which is the shortest book of the Old Testament?
    Ans. Obadiah

Jamaican Heritage

24. Which Jamaican National Hero began his activist career when he volunteered his service as a mediator at Serge Island Estate in 1938?
    Ans. Bustamante

Local and International Affairs

25. What is the name of the man sometimes referred to as the "Oklahoma Bomber"?
    Ans. Timothy McVeigh

Literature

26. Identify the author of the book *How Stella Got Her Groove Back*, which has been made into a movie set mainly in Jamaica.
    Ans. Terry MacMillan

Music

27. In what centuries did the violin-maker Antonio Stradivari live?
    Ans. 17th and 18th

History

28. Who assassinated Martin Luther King, Jr.?
    Ans. James Earl Ray

Mathematics

29. Find the mid-point coordinates of the line joining the points (3, 6) and (7, 5).
    Ans. (5, 5.5)

Sports

30. Name the Brazilian racing driver who died in a car crash in 1994 at the San Marino Grand Prix.
    Ans. Ayrton Senna

Jamaican Heritage

31. Give the maiden name of Edna Manley.
    Ans. Edna Swithenbank

Literature

32. In literature, what is an idyll?
    Ans. A short pastoral poem conveying a mood of happy innocence

Biology

33. What type of joint is there at the ankle?
    Ans. Gliding

Chemistry

34. What is the colour of Mn^{7+} ions in solution?
    Ans. Purple

General Knowledge

35. What name is given to the traditional Afghan veil that covers women from head to toe with a small patch of gauze over the eyes?
    Ans. Burqa

Theatre and Cinema

36. Which Jamaican has played a significant role in the television series *Moesha*?
    Ans. Sheryl Lee Ralph

Geography

37. Which is the highest mountain peak in France?
    Ans. Mount Blanc

Mathematics

38. Factorise $4x^2 - 12x + 9$.
    Ans. $(2x - 3)^2$

Sports

39. How many Jamaicans have won world professional boxing titles?
    Ans. 6

Local and International Affairs

40. With which international organization do you most associate the name Michel Camdesus?
    Ans. The International Monetary Fund (IMF)

Quiz No. 10

I. Alternate Section

Bible Knowledge

1. Which Biblical character said: "Are not two sparrows sold for a farthing?"
   Ans. Jesus

2. In which book of the Bible would you find the line: "I will give you the gold of the land of Egypt and ye shall eat the fat of the land"?
   Ans. Genesis

Mathematics

3. If $a = {}^-3$ and $b = {}^-2$, what is the value of a^3b^2?
   Ans. $^-108$

4. If $a = {}^-9$ and $b = {}^-4$, what is the value of $\frac{a^2}{b^3}$?
   Ans. $-\frac{81}{64}$

English Language

5. Which word means both "a small cube with six faces" and "to cease to live"?
   Ans. Die

6. Which word means both "to search and rob, especially from the pockets" and "a type of firearm, especially one fired from the shoulder"?
   Ans. Rifle

Theatre and Cinema

7. Name the leading male and female performers in the movie *Gone With the Wind*.
   Ans. Clark Gable, Vivian Leigh

8. During which war is the movie *Gone With the Wind* set?
   Ans. The American Civil War

Sports

9. Which was the first horse to win the Triple Crown at Caymanas Park?
   Ans. Royal Dad

10. In each year, which is the last race in the Triple Crown at Caymanas Park?
    Ans. The St. Leger

Biology

11. True or false? Jointed limbs and an exoskeleton are features of animals in the phylum arthropoda.
    Ans. True

12. True or false? Spiny-skinned marine animals belong to the phylum mollusca.
    Ans. False (Echinodermata)

Physics

13. What quality of a body is described as mass per unit volume?

    Ans. Density

14. What is the unit for density in the cgs system?

    Ans. g/cm^3

Art

15. Who sculpted the statue of Norman Manley, located at North Parade in Kingston?

    Ans. Alvin Marriot

16. Who sculpted the statue of the Jamaican athlete located at the National Stadium?

    Ans. Alvin Marriot

Jamaican Heritage

17. For how many years was Spanish Town the capital of Jamaica?

    Ans. 338

18. What was the former name of the Spanish Town Square?

    Ans. The Parade

Music

19. What term is given in music to the short extra lines added above or below the stave to accommodate very high or very low notes?

    Ans. Ledger lines

20. What term is given in music to the distance in pitch between two notes?

    Ans. Interval

Religious Knowledge

21. Which Indian religious festival is called the Festival of Lights?

    Ans. Diwali

22. What name is given to the confirmation ceremony for Jewish boys at age 13?

    Ans. Bar Mitzvah

History

23. Who succeeded Gamel Abdel Nasser as President of Egypt?

    Ans. Anwar Sadat

24. What was Pope John Paul's name before he assumed the papacy?

    Ans. (Cardinal) Karol Wojtyla

General Knowledge

25. Which Latin term denotes the sudden chill with shivering before a fever?

    Ans. *Rigor*

26. What is the meaning of the Latin phrase *rigor mortis*?

    Ans. The stiffening of the body after death

Bible Knowledge

27. In which book of the Bible would you find the line: "The lamp of the body is the eye. If therefore your eye is good, your whole body will be full of light."?

    Ans. Matthew (6:22)

28. Which book of the Bible gives an account concerning Elisabeth and Zechariah?

    Ans. Luke

Geography

29. What is the capital of Bangladesh?

    Ans. Dacca

30. What is the capital of Thailand?

    Ans. Bangkok

Mathematics

31. The capacity of a car park was increased from 40 cars to 45 cars. What was the percentage increase?
     Ans. $12\frac{1}{2}\%$

32. If 30:x is the same as 25:150, what is x?
     Ans. 180

Biology

33. What is the name of the protein released by blood platelets when a blood vessel is damaged and blood is exposed to air?
     Ans. Thrombokinase

34. With which blood protein does Thrombokinase act to form thrombin, in the presence of calcium salts?
     Ans. Prothrombin

Jamaican Heritage

35. Name the place in Portland where the mongoose was first introduced in Jamaica.
     Ans. Spring Garden

36. What was the name popularly given to Jack Mansong, in Jamaica's history?
     Ans. Three Finger Jack

Chemistry

36. The electronic configuration of which element is 2.8.18.8?
     Ans. Krypton

38. The electronic configuration of which ion is 2.8.18.7?
     Ans. Bromine

Mythology

39. Name the wife of Minos, legendary ruler of Crete.
     Ans. Pasiphae

40. Name the bosom friend of Achilles, who fought beside him in the Trojan War.
     Ans. Patroclus

II. The Speed Section

Speed Questions for Team A

1. What is the negative square root of 324?
   Ans. $^-18$

2. Who sculpted the bust of Marcus Garvey located at National Heroes Park?
   Ans. Alvin Marriot

3. What term denotes the energy which a body has by virtue of its position?
   Ans. Potential energy

4. In which parish of Jamaica is the Tamarind Tree Church located?
   Ans. St. Catherine

5. What is the usual colour of copper two plus ions in solution?
   Ans. Blue

6. Give the English equivalent for the Spanish: *Donde humo fuego hay cenizas.*
   Ans. Where there is smoke there is fire.

7. Name the former Chilean President who was arrested in London in 1998 on the warrant of a Spanish court.
   Ans. Augusto Pinochet

8. Which Psalm begins with the line: "Hear this, all you peoples; listen, all who live in this world"?
   Ans. Psalm 49

9. The electronic configuration of which ion is 2.8.6?
   Ans. Sulphur

10. Who wrote the book *How Europe Underdeveloped Africa*?
    Ans. Walter Rodney

11. What term denotes the property of a body which resists a change in its state of rest or of uniform motion?
    Ans. Inertia

12. Which Jamaican won the 400 metres hurdles for men at the 1998 Commonwealth Games?
    Ans. Dinsdale Morgan

13. Spell the word SPAGHETTI.

14. In *Pride and Prejudice*, who eventually marries Elizabeth Bennett?
    Ans. Fitzwilliam Darcy

15. True or false? Mucus is secreted by goblet cells.
    Ans. True

16. What is the meaning of the abbreviation JUTC in Jamaica?
    Ans. Jamaica Urban Transit Company Ltd.

17. From the Latin meaning "go with me", this phrase denotes a handbook or other thing carried constantly about by a person. What is it?
    Ans. *Vade mecum*

18. What is the area of a square if its perimeter is 32 centimetres?
    Ans. 64 square centimetres

19. Name the piece of sculpture which adorns the entrance to the Little Theatre.
    Ans. *Rainbow Serpent*

20. What is the capital of Turkey?
    Ans. Ankara

21. The player of a cembalo would now play which musical instrument?
    Ans. Harpsichord

22. What type of joint is there at the elbow?
    Ans. Hinge

23. What quantity in physics is denoted by displacement divided by time?
    Ans. Velocity

24. The name Sir Clifford Husbands is most associated with which Caribbean country?
    Ans. Barbados

25. Name the longest river in Africa.
    Ans. Nile

26. In what year in the 20th century did Iraq invade Kuwait?
    Ans. 1990

27. In the Bible, who was Solomon's mother?
    Ans. Bathsheba

28. What term is used to describe an illness which is thought to be caused by mental or emotional stress?
    Ans. Psychosomatic

29. Which gas from seawater is used in the experimental apparatus xeta to produce very high temperatures?
    Ans. Deuterium gas

30. What pasture grass came from West Africa to the West Indies?
    Ans. Guinea Grass

31. If x*y is equal to 2x + 3y, what is 2* − 3?
    Ans. ⁻5

32. What is the atomic mass of boron?
    Ans. 11

33. By what name was Vale Royal originally known?
    Ans. Prospect Pen

34. Spell the word PRONUNCIATION.

35. Is blood entering each kidney via the renal artery oxygenated or deoxygenated?
    Ans. Oxygenated

36. In which parish of Jamaica would you find the town of Bangor Ridge?
    Ans. Portland

37. How many West Indian bowlers have taken 8 wickets in one innings of a Test match?
    Ans. 5

38. Give a word ending with the letters "ate" which means to move from side to side, or fluctuate in opinion.
    Ans. Vacillate; oscillate

39. Name the male star of the movie *Taxi Driver*.
    Ans. Robert DeNiro

40. Name the composer, lyricist and playwright who achieved considerable fame with the musical *Oliver*.
    Ans. Lionel Bart

Speed Questions for Team B

1. What is the positive square root of 729?
   Ans. 27

2. Where is Alvin Marriot's statue of Bob Marley located in Kingston?
   Ans. Independence Park

3. What is the potential energy in joules of a body of mass, m, at a point h cm above the ground?
   Ans. mgh/10 J

4. In which Jamaican parish is the Rose Hall Great House located?
   Ans. St. James

5. What is the usual colour of iron two plus ions in solution?
   Ans. Green

6. What is the English equivalent for the Spanish: *Obras son amores, que no buenos razones*?
   Ans. Actions speak louder than words.

7. In what decade of the 20th century did the Falklands War take place?
   Ans. The 1980s

8. Who or what is the *pater noster*?
   Ans. Latin for "Our Father", the opening words of the Lord's Prayer

9. The electronic configuration of which ion is 2.8.8.2?
   Ans. Calcium

10. Who wrote the book *The Myth of Governor Eyre*?
    Ans. Lord Olivier

11. What term denotes the property of an electrical circuit to resist change in the rate or direction of current?
    Ans. Inductance

12. Who is the only Western Hemisphere athlete outside of the USA to win a gold, a silver and a bronze Olympic medal?
    Ans. Donald Quarrie

13. Spell the word STIRRUP.

14. In *A Tale of Two Cities*, who renounces his title and goes to England to live happily with his wife?
    Ans. Charles Darnay

15. True or false? The tube which connects each kidney with the bladder is the ureter.
    Ans. True

16. What is the meaning of the abbreviation TPD Co in Jamaica
    Ans. Tourism Product Development Company

17. Which Latin phrase, meaning "woe to the vanquished", denotes a victor's intention of extracting the full fruits of his victory?
    Ans. *Vae victis*

18. What is the perimeter of a square if its area is 144 square centimetres?
    Ans. 48 centimetres

19. Who sculpted *Rainbow Serpent*?
    Ans. Edna Manley (1975)

20. What is the capital of Lebanon?
    Ans. Beirut

21. Which normal orchestral instrument has the highest pitch?
    Ans. Piccolo or octave flute

22. What type of joint is there at the hip?
    Ans. Ball and socket

23. Which quantity in physics is denoted by distance divided by time?
    Ans. Speed

24. The name Sir Orville Turnquest is most associated with which Caribbean country?
    Ans. The Bahamas

25. Name the longest river in South America.
    Ans. Amazon

26. In what year in the 20th century did the USSR invade Czechoslovakia?
    Ans. 1968

27. In the Bible, who was Cain's first son?
    Ans. Enos

28. What name is given to someone who analyzes handwriting?
    Ans. Graphologist

29. Who appointed the code of symbols for elements and their compounds?
    Ans. Berzelius

30. Which Caribbean island takes its name from the three mountain peaks which are visible from the sea?
    Ans. Trinidad

31. If $x*y = 3x - 3y$, what is $5*6$?
    Ans. $^-3$

32. What is the atomic mass of magnesium?
    Ans. 24

33. What was the original name for the town of Port Antonio?
    Ans. Titchfield

34. Spell the word IMPLEMENTATION.

35. True or false? Mucus lubricates the inside walls of the alimentary canal.
    Ans. True

36. In which parish of Jamaica would you find the town of Pepper?
    Ans. St. Elizabeth

37. Name the two West Indian spin bowlers who have taken 8 wickets in one innings of a Test match.
    Ans. Lance Gibbs and Alfred Valentine

38. Give a word ending with the letters "ate" which means to pervade or saturate.
    Ans. Permeate; penetrate

39. Name the male star of the movie *Saving Private Ryan*.
    Ans. Tom Hanks

40. Who wrote the music for the opera entitled *The Turn of the Screw*?
    Ans. Benjamin Brittain

III. The Signal Section

Literature

1. "Alas, poor Yorick! I knew him, Horatio, a fellow of infinite jest..." said Hamlet, when the gravediggers threw up the skull of the former king's jester. Whose grave were they digging?
   Ans. Ophelia's

Bible Knowledge

2. Identify the biblical king who ordered Shadrach, Meshach and Abednego to be thrown into a fiery furnace.
   Ans. Nebuchadnezzar

Biology

3. With which blood protein does thrombin act to form fibrin?
   Ans. Fibrinogen

Geography

4. Except for about 50 miles of Atlantic coastline to the west, the Gambia is entirely surrounded by which other African country?
   Ans. Senegal

Jamaican Heritage

5. Name the tree at Ferry, St. Catherine which was a landmark in Jamaica for centuries before it was destroyed in the 1960s.
   Ans. Tom Cringle's Cotton Tree

General Knowledge

6. Which Indian rights activist from Guatemala won the Nobel Peace Prize in 1992?
   Ans. Rigoberta Menchu

Mathematics

7. Evaluate 1011 to the base 2 in the decimal system.
   Ans. 11

Sports

8. Which two English football clubs take part in the so-called Merseyside Derby?
   Ans. Everton and Liverpool

History

9. In what century were the Mico Schools first established in the Caribbean?
   Ans. 19th

Biology

10. The embryo in the womb is conferred with protection from the mother's blood. This is an example of which type of immunity?
    Ans. Passive immunity

Local and International Affairs

11. What is the meaning of the abbreviation JSIF?
    Ans. Jamaica Social Investment Fund

Physics

12. Plane polarised light can be obtained by reflecting ordinary white light from the surface of an ordinary glass plate. What is the most suitable angle of incidence for maximum polarisation of the reflected beam: 47, 57 or 67 degrees?
    Ans. 57 degrees

Theatre and Cinema

13. In which film would you hear the line: "Frankly my dear, I don't give a damn"?
    Ans. *Gone with the Wind*

Literature

14. Which West Indian wrote the poem *The Day my Father Died*?
    Ans. Mervyn Morris

Music

15. By what name is the Rap musician born Percy Miller more popularly known?
    Ans. Master P

Sports

16. With which sport do you most associate the name Oscar de la Hoya?
    Ans. Boxing

English Language

17. Give one word which means both "a literary composition" and "to try or test a person or thing".
    Ans. Essay

Art

18. Which 19th century English art critic wrote the books *Seven Lamps of Architecture* and *Stones of Venice*?
    Ans. John Ruskin

Chemistry

19. What term denotes a compound formed by replacing the hydrogen of an acid by a hydrocarbon radical of the ethyl type?
    Ans. An ester

Foreign Languages

20. Give the English equivalent for the Spanish: *Antes que te cases, mira lo que haces*.
    Ans. Look before you leap.

Biology

21. If you had coryza, which organ of your body would be most affected?
    Ans. The nose

Literature

22. Which Shakespearean character said: "The valiant taste of death but once"?
    Ans. Julius Caesar

Jamaican Heritage

23. Who was the only governor of Jamaica to have a public memorial erected to him?
    Ans. Sir Charles Metcalfe

Theatre and Cinema

24. What is the subtitle of the movie "The Lion King II"?
    Ans. Simba's Pride

Sports

25. Who is the only West Indian bowler to take 9 wickets in one innings of a Test match?
    Ans. Jack Noreiga

General Knowledge

26. What would happen to the moon of a planet if it passed the Roche limit?
    Ans. It would break up into fragments.

Art

27. Born 1840, this French painter specialised in open-air subjects, such as Rouen Cathedral, which featured lighting effects achieved by use of broken colour. Name him.
    Ans. Claude Monet

Physics

28. What term in physics denotes the phenomenon that makes liquid rise up a narrow space, as in a fine-bore tube?
    Ans. Capilliarity

Geography

29. What is the capital of Malta?
    Ans. Valetta

Jamaican Heritage

30. In what year was Norman Manley born?
    Ans. 1893

Literature

31. Under what name is Eric Blair more popularly known?
    Ans. George Orwell

General Knowledge

32. How many satellites are known to be in the orbit of the planet Mars?
    Ans. 2

Chemistry

33. What term denotes the process used in the petroleum industry, using a catalyst, in which heavy oil products are split to form lighter ones?
    Ans. Cracking

Biology

34. Is the blood vessel leaving the glomerulus narrower or wider than the one entering it?
    Ans. Narrower

History

35. Who established the Spanish Convoy System?
    Ans. Admiral Pedro Menendez des Aviles

Literature

36. Which West Indian wrote the poems in the anthology entitled *The Pond*?
    Ans. Mervyn Morris

Sports

37. Which English Premier League football team is sometimes called the Magpies?
    Ans. Newcastle

Geography

38. The Hampden and Long Pond Estates are located in which Solution Basin in Jamaica?
    Ans. Queen of Spain's Valley

Physics

39. What is the potential energy of a body of mass 5 kg, 20 metres above the earth's surface?
    Ans. 1000 J

General Knowledge

40. Which German phrase denotes the malicious enjoyment of the misfortune of others?
    Ans. *Schadenfreude*

Quiz No. 11

I. The Alternate Section

Literature

1. "I hold the splendid daylight in my hands,
   Inwardly grateful for a lovely day,
   Thank you life".
   These are the first lines of which poem by a West Indian?
   Ans. *Litany* (by George Campbell)

2. Name the West Indian poet responsible for the following lines:
   "About me young and careless feet
   Linger along the garish street".
   Ans. Claude McKay (*On Broadway*)

Jamaican Heritage

3. Harbour View Housing Estate is located on the site of which old fort?
   Ans. Fort Nugent

4. The ruins of one of the towers of Fort Nugent can be seen in Harbour View today. What is the name of the tower?
   Ans. The Martello Tower

Biology

5. Which layer of the epidermis consists of dead cells which form a tough protective outer coat?
   Ans. The cornified layer

6. Which layer of the epidermis consists of living cells which eventually die and form the cornified layer?
   Ans. The granular layer

Physics

7. A car of mass 2000 kg starts from rest and accelerates uniformly for 10 seconds, reaching a velocity of 20 m/s. What is the acceleration of the car?
   Ans. 2 m/s

8. A car of mass 2000 kg starts from rest and accelerates uniformly for 10 seconds, reaching a velocity of 20 m/s. What is the force acting on the car?
   Ans. 4000 N

English Language

9. Which word ending with the letters "ate" means to sum up or conclude a speech, or to speak at length?
   Ans. Perorate

10. Which word ending with the letters "ate" means lying with the face to the ground?
    Ans. Prostrate

Bible Knowledge

11. Which Psalm begins with the line: "You have rejected us, O God, and burst forth upon us; you have been angry now restore us."?

    Ans. Psalm 60

12. Which Psalm begins with the line: "Have mercy on me, O God, have mercy on me, for in you my soul takes refuge"?

    Ans. Psalm 57

Music

13. Who composed *The Emperor Concerto*?

    Ans. Beethoven

14. Who composed the operas *Orfeo* and *Arianna*?

    Ans. Montiverdi

Mathematics

15. Each interior angle of a regular polygon is 154 degrees. How many sides has the polygon?

    Ans. 10

16. Each interior angle of a regular polygon is 135 degrees. How many sides has the polygon?

    Ans. 8

Geography

17. On which Caribbean island would you find Road Town?

    Ans. Tortola

18. On which continent would you find the city of Islamabad?

    Ans. Asia

Literature

19. Who wrote the Jamaican play *The Runaway*?

    Ans. Carey Robinson

20. Who wrote the play *Ti Jean and his Brothers*?

    Ans. Derek Walcott

Foreign Languages

21. Give the English equivalent to the Spanish: *Mas vale pajaro en mano que ciento volando.*

    Ans. A bird in hand is worth two in the bush.

22. Give the English equivalent to the Spanish: *No se gano Zamora en una hora.*

    Ans. Rome was not built in a day.

Sports

23. Who scored the most goals in the final round of the World Cup football competition in 2002?

    Ans. Ronaldo

24. Who scored Jamaica's first goal in the final round of the World Cup football competition in France in 1998?

    Ans. Robbie Earl

Chemistry

25. What is the atomic mass of potassium?

    Ans. 39

26. What is the atomic mass of sulphur?

    Ans. 32

Music

27. Who was the founder of the French School of Opera?

    Ans. Lully

28. Who is regarded as the founder of the Italian School of Music?
    Ans. Constanzo Festa

Local and International Affairs

29. What is the meaning of the acronym FISH?
    Ans. Foundation for International Self-Help

30. Give the meaning of the acronym CAFRA.
    Ans. Caribbean Association for Feminine Research in Action

Physics

31. In a distance-time graph, describe the action of the object when the graph is a straight line parallel to the x-axis.
    Ans. Stationary

32. In a velocity-time graph, describe the action of the object when the graph is a straight line parallel to the x-axis.
    Ans. Moving with constant velocity

Biology

33. Which tough protective layer surrounds the outside of the eye?
    Ans. The sclerotic layer

34. Which layer of the eye contains black pigmentation which prevents reflection within the eye?
    Ans. Choroid

Foreign Languages

35. Give the English equivalent of the French expression: *Mieux vaut tard que jamais*.
    Ans. Better late than never

36. Give the English equivalent of the French expression: *Aide-toi, le ciel t'aidera*.
    Ans. God helps those who help themselves.

Mythology

37. Which mythical character, son of Priam and Hecuba, was also known as Alexandros?
    Ans. Paris

38. Which hero of Arthurian legend helped restore Amfortas to health, and eventually became guardian of the Holy Grail?
    Ans. Parsifal

Jamaican Heritage

39. In Jamaican heritage, what is shadow catching?
    Ans. Capturing the ghosts of dead people in order to use and control them

40. Which Jamaican cult is most identified with shadow catching, especially at the roots of cotton trees?
    Ans. Myal

II. The Speed Section

Speed Questions for Team A

1. Express 137.051 to 3 significant figures.
   Ans. 137

2. Which organ in the body is concerned primarily with excretion and osmoregulation?
   Ans. Kidney

3. Form an adjective from the word "omen".
   Ans. Ominous

4. In which parish of Jamaica is the town of Porus located?
   Ans. Manchester

5. Which element has atomic number 19?
   Ans. Potassium

6. With which country do you most associate the political name Mahatir Mohammed?
   Ans. Malaysia

7. In mythology, whom did Zeus visit in the form of a shower of gold?
   Ans. Danae

8. At which cricket ground did Brian Lara hit 375 runs in a single innings of a Test match?
   Ans. Antigua Recreational Ground, St. John's

9. Where would you wear a boutonniere?
   Ans. In a buttonhole

10. Of which American State was Bill Clinton once governor?
    Ans. Arkansas

11. Name the lawyer and historian expelled from the PNP in the 1940s, who was readmitted in 1998, after 46 years.
    Ans. Richard Hart

12. Which 15th to 16th century German artist was responsible for engravings entitled *Knight, Death and the Devil*?
    Ans. Albrecht Durer

13. Who wrote the novel *Coningsby*?
    Ans. Benjamin Disraeli

14. Name the first Jamaican footballer to play professionally in Britain.
    Ans. Lindy Delapenha

15. Who is the female star of the 1998 film *Halloween H2O*?
    Ans. Jamie Lee Curtis

16. In which country would you find the city of Liege?
    Ans. Belgium

17. What is the value of $(^-5)^2 + (^-2)^3$?
    Ans. 17

18. Give one word which means "to suspend or attach loosely" and "to suspend a person on a gibbet as capital punishment".
    Ans. Hang

19. What term denotes the ligaments which hold the lens of the eye in place?
    Ans. Suspensory ligaments

20. Which people introduced the pineapple to Jamaica?
    Ans. The Spanish

21. Who composed a comic opera called *The Devil on Two Sticks*?
    Ans. Haydn

22. In oil painting, what term is used for the first coat?
    Ans. Ebauche

23. Give the English equivalent for the Spanish phrase *tener razon*.
    Ans. To be right

24. State the first letter of the Hebrew alphabet.
    Ans. Aleph

25. Complete the Jamaican proverb: "Hawse caan too good fi tie..."
    Ans. "... him own grass."

26. Identify the Jamaican sugar estate used for tourist activities about rum production.
    Ans. Appleton

27. What type of joint is there at the shoulder?
    Ans. Ball and socket

28. What are the factors of $x^2 + 4x - 21$?
    Ans. $(x + 7)(x - 3)$

29. In which group of the periodic table does phosphorus fall?
    Ans. V

30. What award did Horace Burrell receive in the 1998 Jamaican National Honours Ceremony?
    Ans. Order of Distinction (Commander Class)

31. Name the structure in the right atrium which initiates heartbeat.
    Ans. The pacemaker

32. Who was the male star of the movie *Blade*.
    Ans. Wesley Snipes

33. In which African country would you find the Fantee ethnic group?
    Ans. Ghana

34. What alcohol is formed in the fermentation of yeast?
    Ans. Ethanol

35. In what year was Jamaica's National Arena built?
    Ans. 1966

36. Yerevan is the capital of which country?
    Ans. Armenia

37. What is meant by the Latin phrase *res ipsa loquitor*?
    Ans. The thing speaks for itself.

38. In what year did Edward VIII abdicate in Britain?
    Ans. 1936

39. Which element has atomic number 18?
    Ans. Argon

40. Which Psalm begins with the line: "In Judah God is known; his name is great in Israel."?
    Ans. Psalm 76

Speed Questions for Team B

1. Express 137.051 to four significant figures.
   Ans. 137.1

2. What is the normal colour of the kidney?
   Ans. Red-brown

3. Form an adjective from the word "adjective".
   Ans. Adjectival

4. In which parish of Jamaica is the Frome Sugar Estate located?
   Ans. Westmoreland

5. Which element has atomic number 15?
   Ans. Phosphorus

6. With which country do you most associate the political name Alberto Fujimori?
   Ans. Peru

7. In mythology, what event gave rise to the Myrmidons?
   Ans. Zeus turned ants into men.

8. At which cricket ground did Garfield Sobers hit 365 not out in a single innings of a Test match?
   Ans. Sabina Park

9. Which economic class is sometimes denoted by the French term "bourgeoisie"?
   Ans. The middle class

10. For which American State was Hilary Clinton elected senator shortly following the end of her husband's presidency?
    Ans. New York

11. Name the Jamaican who started a soup kitchen with her sister and Edna Manley to feed workers on strike in the Kingston waterfront in 1938.
    Ans. Aggie Bernard

12. Whose painting entitled *Christ in the House of his Parents* aroused controversy when it was first shown?
    Ans. Sir John Everett Millais

13. Who wrote the novel *The Light that Failed*?
    Ans. Rudyard Kipling

14. For which British team did Lindy Delapenha make his first appearance as a professional in Britain in 1948?
    Ans. Portsmouth

15. Who was the female star of the 1998 film *Ever After*?
    Ans. Drew Barrymore

16. In which country would you find the city of Penang?
    Ans. Malaysia

17. What is the value of $2^5 - 2^0$?
    Ans. 31

18. Give one word which means "a stout piece of timber" and "to send in the mail".
    Ans. Post

19. What term denotes the muscles of the eye which hold the suspensory ligaments in place?
    Ans. Ciliary muscles

20. Which people introduced the mango to Jamaica?
    Ans. The English

21. Who composed the oratorio entitled *Israel in Egypt*?
    Ans. Handel

22. In art, what is a nimbus?
    Ans. A halo or circle around the head of a holy figure

23. What part of the body is denoted by the Spanish *la cabeza*?
    Ans. The head

24. State the last letter of the Hebrew alphabet.
    Ans. Taw

25. Complete the Jamaican proverb: "If you put butta gainst puss mouth ..."
    Ans. "... him wi lik it."

26. In which Jamaican parish would you find the scenic attraction known as YS Falls?
    Ans. St. Elizabeth

27. What type of joint is there at the knee?
    Ans. Hinge

28. What are the factors of $x^2 + 5x - 36$?
    Ans. $(x + 9)(x - 4)$

29. In which group of the periodic table does silicon fall?
    Ans. IV

30. What award did Warren Barrett receive in the 1998 Jamaican National Honours Ceremony?
    Ans. Order of Distinction (Officer Class)

31. What is the general term for the maintenance of constant conditions within an organism, such as the control of blood glucose level by insulin?
    Ans. Homeostasis

32. Who was the male star of the movie *Beloved*.
    Ans. Danny Glover

33. What term denotes the prehistoric type of man represented by remains found in China in 1929?
    Ans. Peking Man

34. What gas is given off in the fermentation of yeast?
    Ans. Carbon dioxide

35. Which was the first public event held at the National Stadium?
    Ans. Raising the Jamaican flag

36. Baku is the capital of which country?
    Ans. Azerbaijan

37. What is meant by the Latin phrase *restitutio in integrum*?
    Ans. Restoration to the original position

38. In what year did Nicholas II abdicate in Russia?
    Ans. 1917

39. Which element has atomic number 12?
    Ans. Magnesium

40. Which Psalm begins with the line: "Save me, O God, for the waters have come up to my neck"?
    Ans. Psalm 69

III. The Signal Section

General Knowledge

1. Name the Jamaican who has become a judge on the United Nations International Criminal Tribunal for the former Yugoslavia.
   Ans. Patrick Robinson

Biology

2. What general term denotes the process by which organisms shed their exoskeletons periodically to allow growth?
   Ans. Ecdysis (or moulting)

Theatre and Cinema

3. Give the name of the Jamaican who played the role of Miss Upton in the television series *Lime Tree Lane*.
   Ans. Judith Thompson

Local and Internaional Affairs

4. In 1998, the United States Government commenced an antitrust case against which computer corporation?
   Ans. Microsoft

Proverbs and Idioms

5. Give a well-known idiomatic expression which means to proceed in an object the conclusion of which is well-nigh impossible?
   Ans. To look for a needle in a hay-stack

Sports

6. Which Jamaican boxer defeated the Englishman Dave Charnley to win the Commonwealth lightweight boxing title on the eve of Jamaica's independence?
   Ans. Bunny Grant

Theatre and Cinema

7. For his performance in which film did Marlon Brando win the Academy Award for Best Actor in 1972?
   Ans. *The Godfather*

Bible Knowledge

8. In which book of the Bible would you find the line: "Render unto Caesar the things that are Caesar's and unto God the things that are God's."?
   Ans. Matthew

English Language

9. Give one word which denotes one of the early Germanic peoples and also means "open or candid".
   Ans. Frank

Music

10. Geri Halliwell is a former Spice Girl. Which one?
    Ans. Ginger Spice

History

11. In what century did the Wesleyan Methodists first come to Jamaica?
    Ans. 18th

Local and International Affairs

12. Who succeeded Nelson Mandela as the President of South Africa.
    Ans. Thabo Mbeki

Geography

13. What is the capital of Liechtenstein?
    Ans. Vaduz

Physics

14. When a fluid flows through a tube, at any point the sum of the potential, kinetic and pressure energies is constant. This is a statement of whose principle in physics?
    Ans. Brenoulli's Principle

Theatre and Cinema

15. Which Jamaican wrote the play *The Rope and the Cross*?
    Ans. Easton Lee

Mathematics

16. What is 12.5% of $240?
    Ans. $30

Chemistry

17. In the Bronsted-Laurie Theory, what is the definition of an acid and a base?
    Ans. An acid is a proton donor, a base is a proton acceptor.

Literature

18. Which West Indian wrote the novel *The Chip Chip Gatherers*?
    Ans. Shiva Naipaul

History

20. In what year did Trinidad and Tobago become a joint Crown Colony?
    Ans. 1899

Art

21. Matisse, Rouault, and Vlamick were members of which group of Parisian painters most active in the early 1900s.
    Ans. The Fauves

Mythology

22. Who solved the Riddle of the Sphinx?
    Ans. Oedipus

Local and International Affairs

23. What is the meaning of the abbreviation NIBJ in Jamaica?
    Ans. National Investment Bank of Jamaica

Biology

24. Which part of the brain controls the rate of heartbeat?
    Ans. Medulla oblongata

English Language

25. Give one word which means "a torn or frayed piece of woven material" and "to scold, reprove severely or play rough jokes upon a person".
    Ans. Rag

General Knowledge

26. In which city is the World Intellectual Property Organization located?
    Ans. Geneva

Jamaican Heritage

27. At which corner in Kingston is Gordon House located?
    Ans. Duke and Beeston Streets

Geography

28. In which parish of Jamaica would you find Galina?
    Ans. St. Mary

Literature

29. Which West Indian wrote the poem entitled *Exile*?
    Ans. Dennis Scott

Physics

30. What is the kinetic energy of a body of mass 2 kg with a velocity of 20 m/s?
    Ans. 400 J

Art

31. Born 1853, this Dutch painter who specialised in landscapes and portraits had bouts of insanity and committed suicide in 1890. Name him.
    Ans. Vincent Van Gogh

Literature

32. Under what more popular name do we know the American playwright Thomas Lanier Williams?
    Ans. Tennessee Williams

Chemistry

33. What term denotes the black tarry mixture of high boiling point hydrocarbons which is left behind in the distillation of petroleum?
    Ans. Bitumen

General Knowledge

34. Name the nephew of Charlemagne celebrated in legend often with his comrade Oliver.
    Ans. Roland

English Language

35. Which word means both "a turn of work" or "to write or name the letters that form a word"?
    Ans. Spell

History

36. In what year did John Glenn become the first person to orbit the earth?
    Ans. 1962

Bible Knowledge

37. Which Psalm begins with the line: "Praise awaits you, O God, in Zion"?
    Ans. Psalm 65

Geography

38. What is the capital of California?
    Ans. Sacramento

Mathematics

39. What is the value of $169^{-\frac{1}{2}}$?
    Ans. $\frac{1}{13}$

Local and International Affairs

40. Name any four of the G8 States in international affairs.
    Ans. USA, Japan, Germany, France, Britain, Italy, Canada, Russia

Quiz No. 12

I. Alternate Section

Geography

1. What is the capital of the American State of Wyoming?
   Ans. Cheyenne

2. What is the capital of the American State of Wisconsin?
   Ans. Madison

English Language

3. The root word "clamo" means "I shout". Give two words in which the root is used with this meaning.
   Ans. Clamour, proclaim, exclaim

4. The root word "pendeo" means "I hang". Give two words in which the root is used with this meaning.
   Ans. Depend, suspend, pendant

General Knowledge

5. In which city would you find the secretariat or headquarters of ASEAN?
   Ans. Djakarta, Indonesia

6. In which city would you find the secretariat or headquarters of NATO?
   Ans. Brussels

Religious Knowledge

7. What term, in religion, denotes the belief that inanimate objects (such as rocks), and natural phenomena (such as the wind), have living souls?
   Ans. Animism

8. What term, especially from primitive religion, denotes the attribution of magical powers (or charms) to objects?
   Ans. Fetishism

Theatre and Cinema

9. Name the two actresses who shared the Academy Award for Best Actress in 1968.
   Ans. Katherine Hepburn and Barbara Streisand

10. For her performance in which film did Sally Field win the Academy Award for Best Actress in 1979?
    Ans. Norma Rae

Music

11. In music, what is counterpoint?
    Ans. Two or more melodies combined to form a satisfying harmony

12. What is another term for "counter-tenor" in music?
    Ans. Alto

Literature

13. The poems of which English poet were edited by Siefried Sassoon?
    Ans. Wilfred Owen

14. Name the English Elizabethan playwright who wrote *Tamburlaine the Great*.
    Ans. Christopher Marlowe

Mathematics

15. The area of a trapezium is 63 cm². If the parallel sides are of lengths 3 and 4 centimetres respectively, what is the distance between the parallel sides?
    Ans. 18 cm

16. The area of a trapezium is 42.5 cm². If the parallel sides are of lengths 9 and 10 centimetres respectively, what is the distance between the parallel sides?
    Ans. 5 cm

Physics

17. True or false? A solenoid can be used as an electromagnet.
    Ans. True

18. True or false? Sound is a form of radiation which involves pressure waves in matter.
    Ans. True

Chemistry

19. The element Technetium has two possible valencies. State either one.
    Ans. 6, 7

20. The element Iridium has two possible valencies. State either one.
    Ans. 3, 4

History

21. Which Italian king invited Benito Mussolini to be Prime Minister of Italy in 1922?
    Ans. Victor Emmanuel III

22. Which German president appointed Adolf Hitler Chancellor of Germany in 1933?
    Ans. Paul von Hindenburg

English Language

23. Give another word for "sempiternal".
    Ans. Everlasting

24. Give another word for "vacuous".
    Ans. Empty

Art

25. In what century was the technique of oil painting introduced?
    Ans. 15th century

26. Which artistic pair of brothers first perfected oil painting?
    Ans. The Van Eyck brothers

Biology

27. In biology, what is denoted by the term zoonosis?
    Ans. Infections of animals that may affect man

28. In biology, what is denoted by the term transfusion?
    Ans. Transfer of blood from a healthy individual to an ill one

Foreign Languages

29. Give the meaning of the Spanish *regreso a casa*.
    Ans. He returned home.

30. Give the meaning of the Spanish *volvio a Espana*.
    Ans. He returned to Spain.

Art

31. What is the title of Andrew Wyeth's painting of a woman crawling in a field and looking toward a distant house?
    Ans. *Christina's World*

32. What is the title of the cubist-futurist painting by Marchel Duchamp that caused great controversy when it was exhibited in New York in 1913?
    Ans. *Nude Descending a Staircase*

Foreign Languages

33. What is the meaning of the French term *mal ecrit*?
    Ans. Badly written

34. What is the meaning of the French *l'eau douce*?
    Ans. Fresh water

Local and International Affairs

35. Which organ of the United Nations has as its main objective the maintenance of international peace and security?
    Ans. The Security Council

36. Which branch of the United Nations is responsible under the General Assembly for carrying out functions of the U.N. with regard to international economic, social, cultural, educational and related matters?
    Ans. The Economic and Social Council

General Knowledge

37. In insurance, what is indemnity?
    Ans. Compensation for loss or injury

38. In business, what is a gilt-edged security?
    Ans. The safest type of stock, usually government shares

Bible Knowledge

39. Which Biblical character said the Second Coming would occur "in the twinkling of an eye"?
    Ans. Paul

40. According to the Acts of the Apostles, when Peter and the apostles were taken before the Sanhedrin for the second time, their lives were saved by whose moderating speech?
    Ans. Gamaliel's

II. The Speed Section

Speed Questions for Team A

1. Give the biological name for the skull.
   Ans. The cranium

2. Who preceded Marie Atkins as the mayor of Kingston?
   Ans. Ralph Brown

3. True or false? The fovea of the eye contains many cones.
   Ans. True

4. Give the English equivalent to the Spanish *quien busca halla*.
   Ans. Seek and you shall find.

5. How many satellites does Jupiter have?
   Ans. 16, plus one ring

6. What is the unit of currency in Zimbabwe?
   Ans. Dollar

7. Is Zen a Buddhist or Hindu sect?
   Ans. Buddhist

8. If 8 men dig a ditch in 15 days, how long would it take 10 men to dig the same ditch?
   Ans. 12 days

9. Who won the Oscar for Best Actress in 1980?
   Ans. Cissy Spacek (*Coalminer's Daughter*)

10. Give the meaning of the musical term *allegretto*.
    Ans. At a fairly lively pace

11. In which war did George Orwell fight?
    Ans. The Spanish Civil War

12. Express $\frac{2}{25}$ as a percentage.
    Ans. 8%

13. True or false? Light diffracted by a narrow slit produces a set of diffraction fringes.
    Ans. False (Interference fringes)

14. Which has the higher specific gravity: alcohol or aluminium?
    Ans. Aluminium

15. In what century did Eric the Red visit Greenland?
    Ans. The 10th (982)

16. According to the proverb, what seldom bite?
    Ans. Barking dogs

17. Which artist painted a series of pictures of water lilies?
    Ans. Claude Monet

18. Only one male sprinter has won medals at his third, fourth and fifth Olympic Games. Name him.
    Ans. Donald Quarrie

19. To which phylum does the jellyfish belong?
    Ans. Coelenterata

20. What is the past participle of the Spanish verb *ver*?
    Ans. *Visto*

21. Give the meaning of the French *puis*.
    Ans. Then

22. On the geological time scale, which period came first: the Ordovician or the Silurian period?
    Ans. Ordovician

23. In which city would you find the Commonwealth Secretariat?
    Ans. London

24. Who is the patron saint of policemen?
    Ans. St. Michael

25. Is influenza caused by a virus or a bacterium?
    Ans. Virus

26. By what more popular name do we know the entertainer born Norman Jackson?
    Ans. Tiger

27. Who wrote the poem *Upon Westminster Bridge*?
    Ans. William Wordsworth

28. What is the size of the largest share when $960 is divided in the ratio of 1:2:9?
    Ans. $720

29. What term in physics denotes a force that causes a change of shape?
    Ans. Shear force

30. What is the atomic number of silver?
    Ans. 47

31. Who was the American President at the start of the 20th century?
    Ans. William McKinley

32. Complete the proverb: "A wise man changes his mind sometimes, ..."
    Ans. "...a fool never."

33. With which country do you most associate direct painting?
    Ans. U.S.A.

34. To which class does the crab belong?
    Ans. Crustacea

35. What is the past participle of the Spanish verb *traer*?
    Ans. *Traido*

36. Give the meaning of the French *remarquer*.
    Ans. To notice

37. What is the capital of the American State of West Virginia?
    Ans. Charlestown

38. Which is the main plenary body of the United Nations?
    Ans. The General Assembly

39. According to legend, who converted an entire nation when he interpreted the prophecies of Isaiah for a eunuch?
    Ans. Philip

40. In which period of the periodic table does calcium fall?
    Ans. 4

Speed Questions for Team B

1. Give the biological name for the collar bone.
   Ans. Clavicle

2. Who was the first Vice-Chancellor of the University of the West Indies?
   Ans. Hugh Springer

3. True or false? The fovea of the eye contains many rods.
   Ans. False

4. Give the English equivalent of the Spanish *quien calla otorga*.
   Ans. Silence means consent.

5. How many satellites does Mars have?
   Ans. 2

6. What is the unit of currency in Afghanistan?
   Ans. Aghani

7. In which country was Zen founded: China or Japan?
   Ans. China

8. If 12 men take 7 days to build a wall, how long would it take 4 men to build the same wall?
   Ans. 21 days

9. Who won the Oscar for Best Actress in 1984?
   Ans. Sally Field (*Places in the Heart*)

10. Give the meaning of the musical term *allegro*.
    Ans. At a lively pace

11. In which war did Wilfred Owen die?
    Ans. World War I

12. Express $\frac{8}{12}$ as a percentage.
    Ans. $66\frac{2}{3}\%$

13. True or false? As diffraction depends on wavelength, it cannot lead to dispersion.
    Ans. False

14. Which has the higher specific gravity: pure water or sea water?
    Ans. Sea water

15. In what century did Abel Tasman visit Australia?
    Ans. The 17th (1642)

16. According to the proverb, what is a penny gained?
    Ans. A penny saved

17. Which artist painted a series of pictures of soup cans?
    Ans. Andy Warhol

18. Only one Caribbean player has qualified and played in all of the following: Wimbledon, the US Open, the French Open and the Australian Open. Name him.
    Ans. Richard Russell

19. To which phylum does the rotifer belong?
    Ans. Rotifera

20. What is the past participle of the Spanish verb *venir*?
    Ans. *Venido*

21. Give the meaning of the French word *prochain*.
    Ans. Next, near

116

22. On the geological time scale, which period came first: Proterozoic or Archaeozoic?
    Ans. Archaeozoic

23. In which city would you find the CARICOM Secretariat?
    Ans. Georgetown

24. Who is the patron saint of hunters?
    Ans. St. Hubert

25. Is the blood within the glomerulus under low or high pressure?
    Ans. High

26. By what more popular name do we know the entertainer Rexton Gordon?
    Ans. Shabba Ranks

27. Who wrote the poem *Deserted Village*?
    Ans. Oliver Goldsmith

28. What is the size of the smallest share when $840 is divided in the ratio of 2:3:7?
    Ans. $140

29. What term in physics denotes a low resistance path between two points in a circuit?
    Ans. A short circuit

30. What is the atomic number of molybdenum?
    Ans. 42

31. Who was the American President at the start of the 19th century?
    Ans. John Adams

32. Complete the proverb: "Do not cut off your nose ..."
    Ans. "... to spite your face."

33. In which century was direct painting most popular?
    Ans. 19th

34. To which class does the king crab belong?
    Ans. Merostomata

35. What is the past participle of the Spanish verb *poner*?
    Ans. *Puesto*

36. Give the meaning of the French *servir*.
    Ans. To serve

37. What is the capital of the American State of Washington?
    Ans. Olympia

38. How many judges are there at the International Court of Justice?
    Ans. 15

39. Which Biblical name means "Yahweh has been gracious"?
    Ans. Ananias

40. In which period of the periodic table does chlorine fall?
    Ans. 3

III. The Signal Section

Geography

1. Gabbro is a plutonic rock. What does this mean?
   Ans. It is a rock formed at great depths.

Theatre and Cinema

2. Name the male star of the movie *The Bodyguard From Beijing*.
   Ans. Jet Lee

Jamaican Heritage

3. The former St. Andrew Club in Kingston is now the headquarters of which sporting association?
   Ans. Jamaica Lawn Tennis Association

Biology

4. What term denotes animals whose body temperatures remain fairly constant despite environmental conditions?
   Ans. Homiothermic

Foreign Languages

5. Give the meaning of the French verb *sonner*.
   Ans. To ring

General Knowledge

6. What is the unit of currency in Algeria?
   Ans. Dinar

Bible Knowledge

7. When Philip preached to the Samaritans, he converted many, but when Peter came to confirm their baptism, a convert used the occasion to try to buy apostolic office. Name him.
   Ans. Simon Magus

History

8. Which American poet was charged with treason as a result of his radio broadcasts on behalf of the Italians in World War II?
   Ans. Ezra Pound

Mathematics

9. Find the smallest number that must be added to 7 and 9 to make the L.C.M. 60.
   Ans. 3

General Knowledge

10. In which parish of Jamaica would you find Columbus Park?
    Ans. St. Ann

Physics

11. Convert 41 degrees Fahrenheit to degrees centigrade.
    Ans. 5 degrees centigrade

Chemistry

12. Which has the higher specific gravity: limestone or marble?
    Ans. Marble

History

13. Who defeated the Nawab of Bengal in 1757 at the Battle of Plassey?
   Ans. Robert Clive

English Language

14. Spell the word ADVERSARY.

Art

15. What term denotes the balance of light and shade in a picture?
   Ans. Chiaroscuro

Biology

16. By what other name is Vitamin B_1 known?
   Ans. Thiamine

Jamaican Heritage

17. Which member of the British Royal Family visited Jamaica in February 1996?
   Ans. Princess Margaret

Mathematics

18. Express 0.1342 correct to 3 significant figures.
   Ans. 0.134

Local and International Affairs

19. In what year did Jamaica join the International Monetary Fund: 1963, 1973 or 1983?
   Ans. 1963

Foreign Languages

20. What is the meaning of the Spanish *pasar de*?
   Ans. To exceed

General Knowledge

21. What is the unit of currency in Western Samoa?
   Ans. Tala

History

22. Who succeeded Kurt Waldheim as Secretary-General of the United Nations?
   Ans. Javier Perez de Cuellar

Religious Knowledge

23. What title is given to Muhammed's successors as civil and spiritual leaders?
   Ans. Caliph

Theatre and Cinema

24. Which well-known Jamaican actor wrote the play *Eve*?
   Ans. Oliver Samuels

Music

25. The musician born Pablo Henry is better known by what name?
   Ans. Pablo Moses

Chemistry

26. What is the atomic number of plutonium: 14, 54 or 94?
   Ans. 94

Theatre and Cinema

27. For his performance in which film did George C. Scott receive the Academy Award for Best Actor in 1970?
   Ans. *Patton*

English Language

28. Which word means both "the obscuration of the atmosphere near the earth, mainly due to heat" and "to harass with overwork"?
   Ans. Haze

Art

29. Which Jamaican has a famous painting entitled "Mother and Child"?
    Ans. Barrington Watson

Sports

30. In which city were the Olympic Games held in 1900?
    Ans. Paris

General Knowledge

31. With which country do you associate Varig Airways?
    Ans. Brazil

Mathematics

32. What is the value of $81^{\frac{3}{4}}$?
    Ans. 9

Jamaican Heritage

33. Name the historic building facing Gordon House, which formerly housed the Jamaican legislature.
    Ans. Headquarters House

Physics

34. What is the speed of sound at sea level at 0 degrees centigrade in miles per hour: 252, 532 or 742 m.p.h. ?
    Ans. 742 m.p.h.

Chemistry

35. State the chemical symbol for gallium?
    Ans. Ga

History

36. In what year did Queen Elizabeth II make her first visit to Jamaica?
    Ans. 1953

English Language

37. What is the past participle of the verb "lie"?
    Ans. Lain

Art

38. What term in art denotes a tiny painting, usually a portrait, most often in gouache or water colour.
    Ans. Miniature

Chemistry

39. What type of furnace allows the continuous production of molten iron?
    Ans. A blast furnace

Mathematics

40. If $x^2 + 8x + 15 = 0$ What are the two values of x?
    Ans. $^-3, ^-5$

Quiz No. 13

I. The Alternate Section

Bible Knowledge

1. In the Acts of the Apostles, when Peter was miraculously released from prison, to whose house did he go?
   Ans. The house of Mary, mother of John Mark

2. Name the sorcerer who confronted Paul and Barnabas when they preached the gospel to the proconsul of Paphos.
   Ans. Bar-jesus

Geography

3. In which parish of Jamaica is the town of Ewarton located?
   Ans. St. Catherine

4. In which parish of Jamaica is the town of Walker's Wood located?
   Ans. St. Ann

Theatre and Cinema

5. Who won the Best Actress Oscar in 1985?
   Ans. Geraldine Page (*The Trip to Bountiful*)

6. For her performance in which movie did Emma Thompson win the Academy Award for Best Actress in 1992?
   Ans. *Howard's End*

Music

7. What term denotes opera midway between ballad opera and comic opera?
   Ans. Burletta

8. What term denotes the closing portion of an act or opera, usually a part in which the whole company sings together?
   Ans. Finale

Literature

9. In *The Merchant of Venice*, of what was the casket made that bore the words: "Who chooseth me must give and hazard all he hath"?
   Ans. Lead

10. Which Shakespearean play begins: "In delivering my son from me, I bury a second husband"?
    Ans. *All's Well that Ends Well*

Mathematics

11. What are the factors of $3x^2 - x - 2$?
    Ans. $(3x + 2)(x - 1)$

12. What are the factors of $2x^2 + x - 3$?
    Ans. $(2x + 3)(x - 1)$

Physics

13. When the energy of radiation absorbed in matter causes an electric change, the energy separates electric charges with three possible results or effects. Name them.

    Ans. Photo-emission, photo-conductivity, and the photo-voltaic effect

14. What general name is given to devices based on the photo-electric effects in physics?

    Ans. Photo-cells

Chemistry

15. In the electrochemical series, which has the higher electrode potential: silver or mercury?

    Ans. Silver

16. In the electrochemical series, which has the higher electrode potential: silver or gold?

    Ans. Gold

English Language

17. Give one word which means "complete, total or unqualified" and "to emit audibly a cry or a groan".

    Ans. Utter

18. Give one word which means "a word inserted between lines or in the margin to explain another word or text" and "superficial lustre".

    Ans. Gloss

History

19. In what year was Philippine President Ferdinand Marcos overthrown?

    Ans. 1986

20. Who succeeded Ferdinand Marcos as President of the Philippines?

    Ans. Corazon Aquino

Art

21. Identify the semi-religious group of artists founded in Vienna in 1809, by Overbeck and Pforr.

    Ans. Nazarenes

22. Identify the group of East Anglian painters of the 1700s, including Crome and Cotman.

    Ans. Norwich School

Biology

23. Give the meaning of the biological term "schlerosis".

    Ans. Hardening of any tissue

24. Give the meaning of the biological term "spondylitis".

    Ans. Inflammation of the vertebrae

Foreign Languages

25. Give the meaning of the Spanish *en cuanto*.

    Ans. As soon as

26. Give the meaning of the Spanish verb *secar*.

    Ans. To dry

Local and International Affairs

27. In which city would you find the headquarters of the Organization of American States?

    Ans. Washington D.C.

28. In which city would you find the headquarters of the Organization of African Unity?

    Ans. Addis Ababa

General Knowledge

29. Name the small Indian sect, offshoot of Hinduism in the 6th century B.C., which teaches that salvation depends on rigid self-effort and non-violence.
    Ans. Jainism

30. Name the Persian religion, formed in the 600s B.C., which teaches that morality is the greatest virtue in the battle between good and evil.
    Ans. Zoroastrianism

Music

31. What is the meaning of the musical term *glissando*?
    Ans. Gliding; rapid scales, played with a sliding movement

32. In music, what are grace notes?
    Ans. Ornaments, extra notes added to a melody

Theatre and Cinema

33. Who won the Academy Award for Best Actress in 1969 for her performance in *The Prime of Miss Jean Brodie*?
    Ans. Maggie Smith

34. Who won the Academy Award for Best Actress in 1983 for her performance in *Terms of Endearment*?
    Ans. Shirley MacLaine

Literature

35. In literature, what is a rondeau?
    Ans. A short form of poem, derived from the French, consisting of either 13 or 11 lines, with the first words of the first line used as a refrain.

36. In literature, what is a couplet?
    Ans. Two successive lines of verse that rhyme with one another.

English Language

37. The root word "ruptus" means "broken". Give two words in which the root is used with this meaning.
    Ans. Eruption, interruption, rupture

38. The root word "scribo" means "I write". Give two words in which the root is used with this meaning.
    Ans. Scripture, manuscript, describe

Biology

39. True or false? Rods in the eye are very sensitive to bright light.
    Ans. False

40. True or false? Some cones in the eye are stimulated by light of different wavelengths.
    Ans. True

II. The Speed Section

Speed Questions for Team A

1. What is the value of 0.09 to the power one-half?
   Ans. 0.3

2. How many satellites does Pluto have?
   Ans. 1

3. Which cricketer has the record for the highest aggregate in batting in a single match?
   Ans. Graham Gooch

4. What term denotes the part of the retina where nerve fibres leave the eye and enter the optic nerve?
   Ans. The blind spot

5. On the geological time scale, which period came first: Devonian or Cambrian?
   Ans. Cambrian

6. In Hindu mythology, who is the creator of the world?
   Ans. Brahma

7. For his performance in which film did Robert Duval receive the Academy Award for Best Actor in 1983?
   Ans. *Tender Mercies*

8. Who composed the opera *The Rake's Progress*?
   Ans. Stravinsky

9. What was the nationality of the winner of the Nobel Prize for Literature in 1987, Joseph Brodsky?
   Ans. Russian

10. Express $\frac{1}{12}$ as a percentage.
    Ans. $8\frac{1}{3}\%$

11. State the value of R, the gas constant to 4 decimal places.
    Ans. 8.3143 J/K mol

12. What term denotes the condition in which liquid at very low temperatures flows without friction?
    Ans. Superfluidity

13. In which city would you find the headquarters of the United Nations Development Programme?
    Ans. New York

14. Which battle marked the end of French influence in Indochina?
    Ans. Dien Bien Phu

15. What is the past participle of the verb "lay"?
    Ans. Laid

16. Which member of Jamaica's 1998 football squad to the World Cup has the nickname "Wildboy"?
    Ans. Aaron Lawrence

17. Which West Indian wrote the novel *The Mystic Masseur*?
    Ans. V.S. Naipaul

18. In which period of the periodic table does the element with atomic number 16 fall?
    Ans. 3

20. Name either of the two pioneers of gouache painting in England.
    Ans. Turner; Girtin

21. To which class does the tortoise belong?
    Ans. Reptilia

22. Which Psalm begins with the line: "Vindicate me, O Lord, for I have led a blameless life; I have trusted in the Lord without wavering"?
    Ans. Psalm 26

23. What is the meaning of the Spanish *bonisimo*?
    Ans. Very good

24 Which English football club team has its home ground at Anfield?
    Ans. Liverpool

25. On the geological time scale, which period came first: Jurassic or Permian?
    Ans. Permian

26. Give the meaning of the abbreviation OECD.
    Ans. Organization for Economic Co-operation and Development

27. Is a lama a Hindu or Buddhist priest?
    Ans. Buddhist

28. In which city was Saul baptized into the Christian faith?
    Ans. Damascus

29. Who composed *Piano Concerto in A Minor*?
    Ans. Greig

30. D.H. Lawrence adopted the phoenix as a personal symbol. What bird is named in the title of his first novel?
    Ans. Peacock

31. What is the value of tan 150 degrees?
    Ans. Minus root 3 over 3

32. In which phase of heartbeat do the atria and ventricles relax?
    Ans. Diastole

33. In Buddhism, how many paths are there to Nirvana?
    Ans. 8

34. What is the atomic number of actinium?
    Ans. 89

35. In what year did the Six Day War between Arabs and Israelis take place?
    Ans. 1967

36. What is the past participle of the verb "catch"?
    Ans. Caught

37. What was the nationality of the artist Giotto?
    Ans. Italian (Florentine)

38. How many prime numbers are there between 40 and 50?
    Ans. 3

39. Which cricketer took 14 wickets for 149 runs in a Test match at the Oval, a record for the West Indies?
    Ans. Michael Holding

40. Which part of the body is likely to be affected by the disease impetigo?
    Ans. The skin

Speed Questions for Team B

1. What is the value of 0.4 squared?
   Ans. 0.16

2. How many satellites does Saturn have?
   Ans. 23

3. What is the record for the highest aggregate in batting in a single match?
   Ans. 456 (versus India at Lord's)

4. What term denotes the part of the eye mainly responsible for focusing light on the cells of the retina?
   Ans. The lens

5. On the geological time scale, which period came first: Cretaceous or Triassic?
   Ans. Triassic

6. What is the meaning of the title "Buddha"?
   Ans. Enlightened One

7. For his performance in which film did Peter Finch receive the Academy Award for Best Actor in 1976?
   Ans. *Network*

8. Who composed the opera *The Bartered Bride*?
   Ans. Smetana

9. What was the nationality of the winner of the Nobel Prize for Literature in 1976, Saul Bellow?
   Ans. American

10. Express $\frac{1}{6}$ as a percentage.
    Ans. $16\frac{2}{3}\%$

11. State the value of Avogadro's constant to 5 decimal places.
    Ans. 6.02252×10^{23} per mole

12. Below what temperature in Kelvin does helium exhibit the property of superfluidity?
    Ans. 2.2 K

13. In which city would you find the Golden Gate Bridge?
    Ans. San Francisco

14. In what year did the Battle of Dien Bien Phu take place?
    Ans. 1954

15. What is the past participle of the verb "shake"?
    Ans. Shaken

16. Which former Australian cricketer is nicknamed "Tubbie"?
    Ans. Mark Taylor

17. Which West Indian wrote the novel *Salt*?
    Ans. Earl Lovelace

18. In which period of the periodic table does the element with atomic number 11 fall?
    Ans. 3

19. In medieval times, who or what was a limner in art?
    Ans. A painter of illuminated manuscripts; later a painter of miniatures.

20. To which class does the alligator belong?
    Ans. Crocodilia

21. Which Psalm begins with the line: "Hasten, O God, to save me; O Lord, come quickly to help me."?
    Ans. Psalm 70

22. In which country is Queen Margrethe II the sovereign?
    Ans. Denmark

23. What is the meaning of the Spanish *fatigado*?
    Ans. Tired

24. Which English football club team has its home ground at Goodison Park?
    Ans. Everton

25. On the geological time scale, which period came first: Cambrian or proterozoic?
    Ans. Proterozoic

26. Give the meaning of the abbreviation COMECON.
    Ans. Council for Mutual Economic Aid

27. Is the Bhagavad-Gita a part of the Hindu or Buddhist scriptures?
    Ans. Hindu

28. Who baptized Saul into the Christian faith?
    Ans. Ananias

29. Who composed five *Pomp and Circumstance* marches?
    Ans. Elgar

30. Which poet wrote this epitaph for his own grave: "Cast a cold eye, on life, on death. Horseman, pass by!"?
    Ans. W.B. Yeats

31. What is the value of tan 120 degrees?
    Ans. Minus root 3

32. True or false? In systole, the ventricles contract, forcing blood into the pulmonery artery.
    Ans. True

33. In Buddhism, how many great truths are there?
    Ans. 4

34. What is the atomic number of hafnium?
    Ans. 72

35. In what year did the October War between Arabs and Israelis take place?
    Ans. 1973

36. What is the past participle of the verb "choose"?
    Ans. Chosen

37. What was the nationality of the artist who painted *View of Toledo*?
    Ans. Greek (Cretan, El Greco)

38. With which sport in Jamaica do you most associate the name Marlon Nattie?
    Ans. Basketball

39. How many prime numbers are there between 70 and 80?
    Ans. 3

40. What causes the skin disease impetigo?
    Ans. Staphylococci

III. The Signal Section

Music

1. Name the Spanish cellist, renowned for playing Bach's unaccompanied cello suites, who lived in voluntary exile in Puerto Rico when Franco came to power in Spain.
   Ans. Pablo Casals

Mathematics

2. The length of a rectangle is twice its width. If the area of the rectangle is 50 cm^2, what is the perimeter?
   Ans. 30 cm.

Chemistry

3. What term denotes a substance that flows like a liquid but whose molecules can be arranged in a particular way?
   Ans. Liquid crystal

Physics

4. This is an artificial, short-lived radioactive element made by irradiating Uranium-238 with neutrons, which was first discovered in the debris from the first thermo-nuclear explosion in 1952. Name it.
   Ans. Einsteinium

Literature

5. What literary term denotes a group of three, especially three novels, with a common theme?
   Ans. Trilogy

Religious Knowledge

6. In what year was James I's authorized version of the Bible completed?
   Ans. 1611

English Language

7. Spell the word ELUCIDATE.

Art

8. What is the title of Salvador Dali's painting with a watch hanging limply from the branch of a tree?
   Ans. *Persistence of Memory*

Foreign Languages

9. What is the meaning of the French word *sinon*?
   Ans. If not

Biology

10. Which vitamin helps to prevent beri-beri?
    Ans. Vitamin B^1

Theatre and Cinema

11. For her performance in which film did Marlee Matlin win the Academy Award for Best Actress in 1986?
    Ans. *Children of a Lesser God*

Bible Knowledge

12. According to the Acts of the Apostles, who was the first convert to Christianity in Europe?
    Ans. Lydia

Foreign Languages

13. Give the English equivalent for the Spanish: *A hierro candente, batir de repente.*
    Ans. Strike while the iron is hot.

Music

14. Who composed *The B Minor* symphony?
    Ans. Borodin

Proverbs and Idioms

15. Complete the proverb: "Curses are like chickens, ..."
    Ans. "... they come home to roost."

Mathematics

16. Which trigonometrical function is given by the equation:
    $x - x^3/3! + x^5/5! - x^7/7! ...$?
    Ans. Sin x

Literature

17. Born Francois Marie Arouet, his most famous satirical novel is *Candide*. Name him.
    Ans. Voltaire

Chemistry

18. What are the two valencies of carbon?
    Ans. 2, 4

History

19. In 1887, which African country became engaged in a war with Italy?
    Ans. Ethiopia

Physics

20. What is the kinetic energy of a body of mass 16 kilograms moving with a velocity of 6 metres per second?
    Ans. 288 joules

English Language

21. What is the past participle of the verb "sell"?
    Ans. Sold

Sports

22. Give the name of the book by Robbie Earle about the Jamaican World Cup experience.
    Ans. *One Love* (with Daniel Evans)

Bible Knowledge

23. Which member of the Athenian Council did Paul convert on his mission to Athens?
    Ans. Dionysius

Art

24. Who painted Guernica?
    Ans. Pablo Picasso

Literature

25. Which English poet who settled in the Lake District after his European travels, wrote the poem *The Excursion*?
    Ans. William Wordsworth

Mathematics

26. What is the value of cos 135 degrees?
    Ans. Minus root two over 2

Physics

27. Which photo-electric effect appears with semiconductors?
    Ans. Photo-conductivity

History

28. Between which years did the Russo-Japanese War take place?
    Ans. 1904–1905

Biology

29. To which class does the shark belong?
    Ans. Chondrichthyes

Music

30. Name the rap singer who was released from charges of murder in February 1996.
    Ans. Snoop Doggy Dogg

English Language

31. Give another word for "debonair".
    Ans. Courteous

Mathematics

32. In a class, 25 students do maths and 11 do English. If 10 students do both subjects, how many students do at least one subject?
    Ans. 26

Geography

33. The Appleton Estate is located in which Solution Basin in Jamaica?
    Ans. Appleton

History

34. In Spanish colonial history, what were armadillas and guarda costas?
    Ans. Ships which patrolled colonial waters.

English Language

35. Who or what is a shyster?
    Ans. A person without professional honour, especially a tricky lawyer

Music

36. Give the name of the theme song from the movie *Titanic*.
    Ans. *My Heart Will Go On*

General Knowledge

37. Which country is known as the Land of the White Elephant?
    Ans. Thailand

Sports

38. How many batsmen have scored over 300 runs in a single innings on more than one occasion?
    Ans. One (Bradman, 334 and 304)

Local and International Affairs

39. With which country do you associate the political name Carlos Menem?
    Ans. Argentina

Bible Knowledge

40. Name the second Christian martyr.
    Ans. James, brother of John

Quiz No. 14

I. The Alternate Section

History

1. Approximately how many Indian indentured workers were transported to British Guiana between 1838 and 1917: 139,000; 239,000 or 339,000?
   Ans. 239,000

2. Approximately how many Indian indentured workers were transported to Trinidad between 1838 and 1917: 134,000; 234,000 or 334,000?
   Ans. 134,000

Local and International Affairs

3. Name the comet which became visible from earth in 1997, 4,200 years after its last visit.
   Ans. Hale-Bopp (Next visit: 4397)

4. Name the last British governor of Hong Kong, who gave up office in 1997.
   Ans. Chris Patten

General Knowledge

5. Who was the first Secretary-General of the United Nations?
   Ans. Trygve Lie

6. What was the nationality of Trygve Lie?
   Ans. Norwegian

Geography

7. On which Caribbean island would you find Harrison's Cave?
   Ans. Barbados

8. Which is the most northerly parish in Barbados?
   Ans. St. Lucy

Chemistry

9. What is the oxidation number of nitrogen in $Al(NO_3)^3$?
   Ans. $^+5$

10. What is the oxidation number of chlorine in $KClO_4$?
    Ans. $^+7$

Bible Knowledge

11. In which book of the Bible would you find the line: "Children, obey your parents in the Lord."?
    Ans. Ephesians (6:1)

12. In which book of the Bible would you find the line: "And a little child shall lead them."?
    Ans. Isaiah (11:6)

Foreign Languages

13. What is the meaning of the Spanish sentence: *El es como un hermano*?
    Ans. He is like a brother.

14. What is the meaning of the Spanish sentence: *Le gusta jugar al futbol*?
    Ans. He likes playing football.

Theatre and Cinema

15. Who played the role of Marcia, a struggling single mother, in the movie *Dance Hall Queen*?
    Ans. Audrey Reid

16. Who played the role of villain and executioner in the movie *Dance Hall Queen*?
    Ans. Paul Campbell

Mathematics

17. If $\frac{3}{4}$ of a sum of money is subtracted from $\frac{7}{8}$ of the sum of money, the remainder is $8. What is the sum of money?
    Ans. $64

18. If $\frac{1}{2}$ of a sum of money is subtracted from $\frac{3}{4}$ of the sum of money, the remainder is $96. What is the sum of money?
    Ans. $384

History

19. Who wrote the 19th century historical work *A Twelvemonth's Residence in the West Indies*?
    Ans. R.R. Madden

20. Who wrote the 19th century historical work *The Ordeal of Free Labour in the British West Indies*?
    Ans. W.G. Sewell

Physics

21. A circuit consists of a 2 ohm resistor and a 3 ohm resistor in parallel. A 3 volt battery is connected to the circuit. How big a current is drawn from it?
    Ans. 2.5 amperes

22. A circuit consists of a 3 ohm resistor and a 4 ohm resistor in parallel. A 4 volt battery is connected to the circuit. How big a current is drawn from it?
    Ans. $6\frac{6}{7}$ amperes

Foreign Languages

23. Give the meaning of the French verb *oublier*.
    Ans. To forget

24. Give the meaning of the French verb *partager*.
    Ans. To share

Art

25. Which Venetian artist, whose nickname means "little dyer", is regarded as the last great artist of the Renaissance?
    Ans. Tintoretto

26. What name was Tintoretto given at birth?
    Ans. Jacopo Robusti

Biology

27. Excluding the caudal or tail region, how many vertebrae are there in the vertebral column?
    Ans. 29

28. In the body, what is the function of the neural spine of each vertebra?
    Ans. For the attachment of muscles which bend or straighten the whole vertebral column

Sports

29. FITA is the governing body of which sport?
    Ans. Archery

30. The modern rules for which game were first codified in Poona, India in 1876?
    Ans. Badminton

Geography

31. What is the meaning of the place name Addis Ababa?
    Ans. New Flower

32. What is the meaning of the place name Tierra del Fuego?
    Ans. Land of fire

Literature

33. What literary term denotes a novel based upon actual people under disguised names?
    Ans. Roman-à-clef

34. Give one word which denotes fiction depicting the moral and intellectual growth of a protagonist, often intended for the education and guidance of others.
    Ans. Bildungsroman

Chemistry

35. Which element has atomic number 14?
    Ans. Silicon

36. Which element has atomic number 74?
    Ans. Tungsten

Biology

37. Which psychiatric condition denotes a psychosis in which the patient suffers from delusions of persecution?
    Ans. Paranoia

38. Which psychiatric condition denotes a state of feeling in which the patient feels set apart from either himself or others?
    Ans. Alienation

General Knowledge

39. Which former Caribbean head of government had the middle name "Bharrat"?
    Ans. Cheddi Jagan

40. Which former Caribbean head of government had the middle name "Linden"?
    Ans. Forbes Burnham

II. The Speed Section

Speed Questions for Team A

1. In which country was Mother Theresa born?
   Ans. Albania

2. What computer term denotes the production of an arithmetical result greater than the capacity of the result field?
   Ans. Overflow

3. Give one word for a morbid fear of animals.
   Ans. Zoophobia

4. With which sport do you associate the name Linton McKenzie?
   Ans. Athletics (long-distance running)

5. Give the meaning of the French verb *meriter.*
   Ans. To deserve

6. Who won the Nobel Prize for Literature in 1997?
   Ans. Dario Fo

7. What is the meaning of the word "corpulent"?
   Ans. Fat

8. A nicitating membrane is present in many vertebrates. What is it?
   Ans. A third eyelid

9. In what year did Courtney Walsh make his Test debut: 1974, 1984 or 1994?
   Ans. 1984

10. What is the probability of drawing an ace or a king from a standard pack of playing cards?
    Ans. $\frac{1}{26}$

11. Which country recently unveiled what is believed to be the world's oldest metal statue?
    Ans. Egypt

12. Which political leader dissolved the British Parliament in 1655?
    Ans. Oliver Cromwell

13. The Cartwright rules, introduced in New Jersey in 1846, govern which modern sport?
    Ans. Baseball

14. Give the meaning of the abbreviation HIV.
    Ans. Human immunodeficiency virus

15. Who wrote the novel *Lucky Jim*?
    Ans. Kingley Amis

16. In which book of the Bible would you find the line: "Can the Ethiopian change his skin, or the leopard his spots?"?
    Ans. Jeremiah (13:23)

17. Give the year in which Sir Francis Drake captured Cartegena on his "Indies Voyage".
    Ans. 1586

18. Name the two land-locked countries of South America.
    Ans. Paraguay and Bolivia

19. A circuit consists of two 5 ohm resistors in parallel. What is the effective resistance of the circuit?
    Ans. 2.5 amperes

20. Which is the smallest living bird?
    Ans. The hummingbird

21. Which Jamaican organization is abbreviated as the NFPB?
    Ans. The National Family Planning Board

22. What is the positive value of $(\frac{9}{144})^{-\frac{1}{2}}$?
    Ans. 4

23. Give the name of the first black player to represent South Africa in international cricket.
    Ans. Makhaya Ntini

24. Is acidified potassium manganate a common oxidising or reducing agent?
    Ans. Oxidising agent

25. With which political party in Northern Ireland do you associate the name Gerry Adams?
    Ans. Sinn Fein

26. What name was DJ Beenie Man given at birth?
    Ans. Moses Davis

27. This country is unique in that it is situated in two continents, Asia and Europe. The dividing line is the Bosphorus. Name the country.
    Ans. Turkey

28. Evaluate 7 divided by 4 tan 0.
    Ans. Infinity

29. Identify the novelist who wrote *Erewhon*.
    Ans. Samuel Beckett

30. Which organism causes plague?
    Ans. Pasteurella pestis

31. Which United Nations agency is abbreviated as the WMO?
    Ans. World Meteorological Organization

32. State the factors of $x^2 + x - 12$.
    Ans. $(x - 3)(x + 4)$

33. Which Nigerian wrote the book *The Open Sore of a Continent* about his country?
    Ans. Wole Soyinka

34. What is the atomic number of thallium: 71, 81 or 91?
    Ans. 81

35. Which psychiatric condition denotes an irrational fear, often in response to an unrecognized stimulus?
    Ans. Anxiety

36. Is Madagascar located off the east or west coast of Africa?
    Ans. East coast

37. How many members are there on a baseball team?
    Ans. 9

38. What is the oxidation number of hydrogen in the hydrogen (H^+) ion?
    Ans. $^{+}1$

39. Give the English equivalent of the Spanish *del col a sol*.
    Ans. From dawn to dusk

40. Which police force is referred to as the "watchdogs of the Prairies"?
    Ans. The Royal Canadian Mounted Police

Speed Questions for Team B

1. Of which country was Mother Theresa a citizen at the time of her death?
   Ans. India

2. What computer term denotes the complete sequence of instructions for steps for a job to be performed by computer?
   Ans. Program

3. Give one word for a morbid fear of spiders.
   Ans. Arachnophobia

4. In which Jamaican parish does the 10 kilometre High Mountain Coffee Road Race take place annually?
   Ans. Manchester

5. Give the meaning of the French verb *nager*.
   Ans. To swim

6. What is the nationality of Dario Fo, the 1997 Nobel Laureate for Literature?
   Ans. Italian

7. What is the meaning of the word "opulent"?
   Ans. Wealthy

8. What is the smallest mammal?
   Ans. The bat

9. What was the nationality at birth of the former West Indies cricket captain Frank Worrell?
   Ans. Barbadian

10. What is the probability of drawing a heart or a diamond from a standard pack of playing cards?
    Ans. $\frac{1}{2}$

11. Which Egyptian is the subject of what is believed to be the world's oldest metal statue?
    Ans. Pharaoh Pepy I

12. In which country was there a "Bloody Sunday" massacre in 1905?
    Ans. Russia

13. The winners of the American League and the National League in United States baseball challenge each other in which competition?
    Ans. World Series

14. Give the meaning of the abbreviation SACTF.
    Ans. Special Anti-Crime Task Force

15. Who wrote the novel *Lorna Doone*?
    Ans. R.R. Blackmore

16. In which book of the Bible would you find the line: "Behold, a virgin shall conceive, and bear a son, and shall call his name Immanuel."?
    Ans. Isaiah (7:14)

17. Give the year in which the Battle of the Saints took place?
    Ans. 1782

18. Name the Central American country which is unique in that it has no standing army.
    Ans. Costa Rica

19. A circuit consists of a 4 ohm resistor and a 5 ohm resistor in parallel. What is the effective resistance of the circuit?
    Ans. $2\frac{2}{9}$ amperes

20. Which is the largest living bird?
    Ans. The ostrich

21. Give the meaning of the abbreviation UTASP in Jamaica.
    Ans. Union of Technical, Administrative and Supervisory Personnel

22. What is the positive value of $(\frac{8}{27})^{\frac{1}{3}}$?
    Ans. $\frac{2}{3}$

23. With which sport do you associate the term "double bogey"?
    Ans. Golf

24. Is acidified potassium dichromate a common oxidising or reducing agent?
    Ans. Oxidising agent

25. With which European country do you most associate the name Jean-Marie Le Pen?
    Ans. France

26. Which Jamaican entertainer is sometimes described as the "Cool Ruler"?
    Ans. Gregory Isaacs

27. Name the two seas connected by the Bosphorus.
    Ans. Black Sea and the Sea of Marmara

28. Evaluate tan 60 multiplied by tan 30.
    Ans. 1

29. Identify the novelist who wrote *The Innocence of Father Brown*.
    Ans. G.K. Chesterton

30. What do haversian canals carry?
    Ans. Blood vessels and nerves through bone

31. Which United Nations agency is abbreviated as the IFC?
    Ans. The International Finance Corporation

32. State the factors of $x^2 + x - 42$.
    Ans. $(x - 6)(x + 7)$

33. Which Kenyan wrote the book *Petals of Blood*?
    Ans. Ngugi Wa Thiongo

34. What is the atomic number of thorium: 70, 80 or 90?
    Ans. 90

35. Which psychiatric term denotes a fixed idea, held by a patient, that is at variance with the beliefs and ideas held by normal people?
    Ans. Delusion

36. Freetown is the capital of which African State?
    Ans. Sierra Leone

37. Which modern game was devised by James Naismith in Massachusetts in 1891?
    Ans. Basketball

38. What is the oxidation number of magnesium in magnesium metal?
    Ans. 0

39. Give the English equivalent of the Spanish: *Saltar de la sarten y dar en las brazas*.
    Ans. To jump from the frying pan into the fire

40. Which state of the USA is sometimes referred to as the Blue Grass State?
    Ans. Kentucky

III. The Signal Section

Literature

1. Who wrote *The Sound and the Fury*?
   Ans. William Faulkner

Physics

2. The electrical energy produced by a Leclanche cell is derived from the reaction between zinc and ammonium chloride. True or False?
   Ans. True

General Knowledge

3. Give one word which denotes the complete performance of a computer program, as well as to travel hurriedly.
   Ans. Run

Biology

4. Which part of the brain is chiefly responsible for balance and the co-ordination of muscular activity?
   Ans. Cerebellum

History

5. For how many years did Britain hold Hong Kong as a colony?
   Ans. 156

Local and International Affairs

6. Name the woman who has brought a sexual harassment suit against President Clinton in the United States of America.
   Ans. Paula Jones

Chemistry

7. Which of the following is an electrolyte: sugar solution, mercury, ethyl alcohol or silver nitrate solution?
   Ans. Silver nitrate solution

Foreign Languages

8. Translate the Spanish sentence: A *Juanne le gustan los legumbres*.
   Ans. John does not like vegetables.

Sports

9. In what year was basketball introduced as an Olympic Sport for men: 1936, 1956 or 1976?
   Ans. 1936 (for men); 1976 (for women)

Mathematics

10. State the value of 111_4 as a denary number.
    Ans. 21

Bible Knowledge

11. Which apostle witnessed the martyrdom of Stephen?
    Ans. Paul

General Knowledge

12. Which secretary to the Admiralty in England became famous for his "Diary" covering the period from 1660 to 1669?
    Ans. Samuel Pepys

Music

13. Which Jamaican entertainer had a hit single in the 1990s entitled "Fly de Gate"?
    Ans. Bionic Steve

English Language

14. Spell the word VICISSITUDE.

Art

15. In art, what is a conversation piece?
    Ans. A type of portrait painting that included two or more people (usually of the same family) informally or casually posed.

Geography

16. What is the capital of the largest country in Central America?
    Ans. Managua, Nicaragua

Literature

17. Who wrote the novel *Joseph Andrews*?
    Ans. Henry Fielding

History

18. In which South American country was there a so-called "Dirty War" in the period 1976–83?
    Ans. Argentina

Jamaican Heritage

19. In the name of the broadcasting house RJR, what was the meaning of the second "R"?
    Ans. Rediffusion

Biology

20. Which is the largest order in the animal kingdom?
    Ans. Beetles

General Knowledge

21. Which chemist is said to have founded nutrition as a science?
    Ans. Antoine Lavoisier

Bible Knowledge

22. Where did Moses receive the Ten Commandments?
    Ans. Mount Sinai

Chemistry

23. Is household bleach (sodium chlorate) a common oxidising or reducing agent?
    Ans. Oxidising

Local and International Affairs

24. In 1997, Marshall Applewhite and about 40 adherents of which cult committed suicide as a group?
    Ans. The Heaven's Gate cult

Literature

25. Who wrote the book *Roots*?
    Ans. Alex Haley

Foreign Languages

26. Give the meaning of the French verb *payer*.
    Ans. To pay for

General Knowledge

27. In which country could you receive the Order of Good Hope as a national honour?
    Ans. South Africa

Music

28. In opera, what term denotes male roles sung by women, sometimes called breeches roles?
    Ans. Travesti

Literature

29. Who wrote the book *The Turn of the Screw*?

    Ans. Henry James

Biology

30. Is herpes zoster caused by a virus or a bacterium?

    Ans. Virus

Foreign Languages

31. Give the meaning of the French verb *quitter*.

    Ans. To leave

English Language

32. What is the past participle of the verb "tear"?

    Ans. Torn

Mathematics

33. Factorise $4x^2 - 4x + 1$.

    Ans. $(2x - 1)^2$

Sports

34. In which city were the Olympic Games held in 1968?

    Ans. Mexico City

Chemistry

35. State the chemical symbol for Curium?

    Ans. Cm

Music

36. Is contralto a high or low female voice?

    Ans. Low female voice

History

37. Who served as British Prime Minister from 1976 to 1979?

    Ans. James Callaghan

Theatre and Cinema

38. Name either of the two male stars in the movie *Heat*.

    Ans. Al Pacino; Robert DeNiro

Art

39. What term in art denotes the thick laying on of paint on canvas or wood?

    Ans. Impasto

Local and International Affairs

40. With which country do you associate the political name Eduardo Frei?

    Ans. Chile

Quiz No. 15

I. The Alternate Section

General Knowledge

1. In which African country would you find the Seshamani Land Grant?
   Ans. Ethiopia

2. Name the leader who was responsible for establishing the Seshamani Land Grant.
   Ans. Emperor Haile Selassie

Bible Knowledge

3. Which Psalm begins with the line: "The heavens declare the glory of God; and the firmament sheweth his handywork."?
   Ans. Psalm 19

4. Which Psalm begins with the line: "O Lord God of my salvation, I have cried day and night before thee"?
   Ans. Psalm 88

Literature

5. Which West Indian, who was once a staff writer for the New Yorker magazine, wrote the novel, *The Autobiography of my Mother*?
   Ans. Jamaica Kincaid

6. Give the name of the largely autobiographical novel by Jamaica Kincaid published in 1990?
   Ans. *Lucy*

Chemistry

7. Which one of the following gases does not obey Henry's law fairly closely: hydrogen chloride, carbon monoxide or argon?
   Ans. Hydrogen chloride

8. The mass of gas which dissolves in a fixed volume of liquid does not depend on which of the following: the pressure of the gas, Le Chatelier's Principle or the temperature of the liquid?
   Ans. Le Chatelier's Principle

Mathematics

9. What are the factors of $4x^2 + 13x + 3$?
   Ans. $(4x + 1)(x + 3)$

10. What are the factors of $3x^2 + 5x + 2$?
    Ans. $(3x + 2)(x + 1)$

History

11. In what year was the Missouri Compromise concerning slavery reached in the United States of America?
    Ans. 1820

12. In what year was the Dred Scott decision concerning slavery reached by the American Supreme Court?
     Ans. 1857

Biology

13. What is meant, in biology, by the Placebo effect?
     Ans. Getting better after taking a "dummy" drug

14. What is meant, in biology, by withdrawal symptoms?
     Ans. The body's readjustment after being cut off from a habit-forming substance

English Language

15. Distinguish between the words "momentous" and "momentary".
     Ans. "Momentous" means of very great importance; "momentary" means lasting only for a moment.

16. Distinguish between the words "elegy" and "eulogy".
     Ans. An elegy is a poem of sorrow for the dead; a eulogy is high praise, written or spoken, usually of a dead person.

Physics

17. True or false? 22.4 litres at 0 degrees centigrade and 1 atmosphere pressure is the volume occupied by 1 mole of hydrogen.
     Ans. True

18. True or false? 22.4 litres at 0 degrees centigrade and 1 atmosphere pressure is the volume occupied by 32.0 grammes of oxygen.
     Ans. True

General Knowledge

19. What is the local name given to Diamond Island, a steep-sided islet in the Caribbean?
     Ans. Kick-em-Jenny

20. Which Caribbean state has sovereignty over Kick-em-Jenny?
     Ans. Grenada

Physics

21. What is the value of Avogadro's constant to five decimal places?
     Ans. 6.02252×10^{23} per mole

22. What is the value of Planck's constant to four decimal places?
     Ans. 6.6256×10^{-34} J s

Geography

23. True or false? The US Virgin Islands have never been considered as part of the Leeward Islands?
     Ans. True

24. True or false? The Islands of St. Eustatius, Saba and part of St. Martin are known as the Windward Island group of the Netherland Antilles?
     Ans. True

Foreign Languages

25. What is the English equivalent for the Spanish phrase *el sol poniente*?
     Ans. The setting sun

26. What is the English equivalent for the Spanish phrase *el agua corriente*?
     Ans. Running water

History

27. Who was the first Chancellor of the University of the West Indies?
     Ans. Princess Alice

28. The Mona Campus of the UWI is located on an area of land leased from the Government of Jamaica for how many years?
   Ans. 999

Mathematics

29. If $\frac{1}{2}$ of my money is subtracted from $\frac{2}{3}$ of the money, the result is $24. How much is the total sum of money?
   Ans. $144

30. If $\frac{1}{3}$ of my money is subtracted from $\frac{1}{2}$ of the money, the result is $32. How much is the total sum of money?
   Ans. $192

General Knowledge

31. With which country do you associate the 20th century political leader Konrad Adenaeur?
   Ans. West Germany

32. With which country do you associate the 20th century political leader Zulfikar Ali Bhutto?
   Ans. Pakistan

Theatre and Cinema

33. The movie *Man on the Moon* was based on the life of which American comedian?
   Ans. Andy Kaufman

34. Name the star of the movie *Man on the Moon*.
   Ans. Jim Carrey

Sports

35. With which sport do you associate the Hopman Cup?
   Ans. Tennis

36. What is the nationality of the tennis player Anna Kournikova?
   Ans. Russian

Mythology

37. Which mythological character was the offspring of Pasiphae and a beautiful bull?
   Ans. Minos

38. Which mythological character constructed the Labyrinth?
   Ans. Daedalus

History

39. Who proclaimed himself emperor of Haiti in 1804?
   Ans. Dessalines

40. Who succeeded Dessalines as emperor in the north of Haiti in 1807?
   Ans. Christophe

II. The Speed Section

Speed Questions for Team A

1. What is the tangent of 60 degrees?
    Ans. Root 3

2. Give one word for an instrument for measuring altitudes.
    Ans. Altimeter

3. Which liver disease is associated with poor hygiene, hepatitis A or B?
    Ans. A

4. Which European artist painted *Giovanni Arnolfini and his Bride Hermes*?
    Ans. Jan van Eyck

5. Who wrote the book *The Pearl*?
    Ans. John Steinbeck

6. What is the atomic number of lutetium?
    Ans. 71

7. In which Shakespearean play does the character Polonius appear?
    Ans. Hamlet

8. What is the SI unit of radiant flux?
    Ans. Watt

9. Which singers had a major hit in 1996 with *One Sweet Day*?
    Ans. Mariah Carey and Boyz II Men

10. Evaluate 64 squared minus 36 squared.
    Ans. 2800

11. Complete the Jamaican proverb "A noh wan time monkey ..."
    Ans. "... waan wife."

12. In what year did Wilhelm Roentgen discover x-rays?
    Ans. 1895

13. Which book of the Bible follows 2nd Samuel?
    Ans. 1st Kings

14. Name the strait between Australia and the island of Tasmania.
    Ans. Bass Strait

15. Give the meaning of the Spanish verb *simular*.
    Ans. To pretend

16. In which country did an African war of independence against France begin in 1954?
    Ans. Algeria

17. What is the meaning of the word "urban"?
    Ans. Pertaining to the city or town

18. Into which ocean does the Orinoco flow?
    Ans. Atlantic

19. What is the kinetic energy of a body of mass 1 kilogram moving with a velocity of 1 metre per second?
    Ans. $\frac{1}{2}$ joule

20. Which West Indian wrote the novel *Genesis of the Clowns*?
    Ans. Wilson Harris

21. Name the first official Governor of Tortuga.
    Ans. Bertrand D'Ogeron

22. What is the meaning of the French verb *saluer*?
    Ans. To greet

23. What name is given by Akan-speaking people to a girl child born on Saturday?
    Ans. Mimba

24. Which classical composer is noted for composing over 500 harpsichord sonatas?
    Ans. Scarlatti

25. Which actress played the role of Cleopatra Jones in the movie of the same name?
    Ans. Tamara Dobson

26. Which has the higher specific gravity: alcohol or pitch?
    Ans. Pitch

27. What is the French for "Thursday"?
    Ans. *Jeudi*

28. Name the pituitary hormone that stimulates uterine contractions and milk production at birth.
    Ans. Oxytocin

29. What is the simple interest on $320 for 2 years at 5 per cent per annum?
    Ans. $32

30. Who wrote the book *The Grass is Singing*?
    Ans. Doris Lessing

31. Pronounce the word spelt M-A-L-I-G-N.

32. What are the two valencies of mercury?
    Ans. 1 and 2

33. Which singing group had a major hit entitled *Night Fever* in 1978?
    Ans. Bee Gees

34. In what year was the Treaty of Cateau-Cambresis signed?
    Ans. 1559

35. What is the meaning of the Spanish *la mitad*?
    Ans. Half

36. Which European artist painted *Madonna of the Harpies*?
    Ans. Del Sarto

37. Which Jamaican poet was once secretary to Emperor Haile Selassie?
    Ans. Una Marson

38. By which treaty did the British receive the Spanish asiento for thirty years from 1713?
    Ans. Utrecht

39. Give the name of the central character in Washington Irving's most popular story.
    Ans. Rip Van Winkle

40. The geographical term "Karst" takes its name from a barren region on the coast of which sea?
    Ans. The Adriatic

Speed Questions for Team B

1. What is the sine of 0 degrees?
   Ans. 0

2. Give one word for an instrument for detecting earthquakes.
   Ans. Seismograph

3. Which type of herpes virus causes genital sores, herpes simplex type 1 or type 2?
   Ans. Type 2

4. Which European artist painted *Jupiter and Io*?
   Ans. Correggio

5. Who wrote the book *Shane*?
   Ans. Jack Schaeffer

6. What is the atomic number of thulium?
   Ans. 69

7. In which Shakespearean play does the character Portia appear?
   Ans. *The Merchant of Venice*

8. What is the SI unit for the quantity of heat?
   Ans. Joule

9. Which singing group had a major hit in 1968 with *Hey Jude*?
   Ans. The Beatles

10. Evaluate 92 squared minus 8 squared.
    Ans. 8400

11. Complete the Jamaican proverb "Seb'n bredda ..."
    Ans. "... seb'n diffrant mine."

12. In what year did Van Allen discover radiation belts surrounding the earth?
    Ans. 1958

13. Which book of the Bible follows 2nd Chronicles?
    Ans. Ezra

14. Name the strait between the two main islands of New Zealand.
    Ans. Cook Strait

15. Give the meaning of the Spanish verb *sostener*.
    Ans. To maintain

16. Within one month of which African country's independence did its province of Katanga secede in 1960?
    Ans. The Congo

17. What is the meaning of the word "debar"?
    Ans. To shut out; to prohibit

18. In which country does the Orinoco River rise?
    Ans. Venezuela

19. What is the kinetic energy of a body of mass 2 kilograms moving with a velocity of 2 metres per second?
    Ans. 4 joules

20. Which West Indian wrote the novel *Christopher*?
    Ans. Geoffrey Drayton

21. Name the wealthy merchant who supported Thomas Warner's early settlement efforts in St. Kitts.
    Ans. Ralph Merrifield

22. What is the meaning of the French verb *lire*?
    Ans. To read

23. What name is given by Akan-speaking people to a girl child born on Wednesday?
    Ans. Cuba

24. Which classical composer is noted for preparing musical notation and the terminology of "do, re mi"?
    Ans. Guide d'Arezzo

25. Which musician was responsible for the award-winning soundtrack for the movie "Shaft"?
    Ans. Isaac Hayes

26. Which has the higher specific gravity: limestone or marble?
    Ans. Marble

27. What is the French for "Wednesday"?
    Ans. *Mercredi*

28. Name the pituitary hormone that stimulates milk production after birth.
    Ans. Prolactin

29. What is the simple interest on $480 for 3 years at 2 per cent per annum?
    Ans. $28.80

30. Who wrote the book *The 39 Steps*?
    Ans. John Buchan

31. Pronounce the word spelt I-N-D-I-C-T.

32. What are the two valencies of iron?
    Ans. 2 and 3

33. Which duo had a major hit entitled *Endless Love* in the late 1970s?
    Ans. Diana Ross and Lionel Ritchie

34. In what year was the Edict of Nantes promulgated?
    Ans. 1598

35. What is the meaning of the Spanish *a solas*?
    Ans. Alone

36. Which European artist painted *Vision of St. Bernard*?
    Ans. Filippino Lippi

37. Which Jamaican poet wrote the poems in the anthology *Examination Centre*?
    Ans. Mervyn Morris

38. Which treaty marked the end of the War of Captain Jenkins Ear in 1748?
    Ans. Treaty of Aix-la-Chapelle

39. Give the name of the brooding master of Thornfield Manor in *Jane Eyre*.
    Ans. Mr. Rochester

40. The area known as Landes in southern France is noted for which geographical feature?
    Ans. Sand dunes

III. The Signal Section

History

1. "Still in thought as free as ever, What are England's rights, I ask, Me from my delights to sever, Me to torture, me to task?" Who wrote these words in the poem *The Negro's Complaint*?
   Ans. Cowper

Literature

2. Who wrote the novel *The View From Coyaba*?
   Ans. Peter Abrahams

Physics

3. Which has the greater rest mass, the proton or the neutron?
   Ans. Neutron

English Language

4. Spell the word ACRIMONIOUS.

General Knowledge

5. Give an 11-letter word which denotes the Chinese form of medical treatment using long needles.
   Ans. Acupuncture

Chemistry

6. The element with atomic weight 106.4 has the chemical symbol Pd. Name it.
   Ans. Palladium

Music

7. In what year did the Grammy Awards include a Reggae category for the first time?
   Ans. 1985

Foreign Languages

8. Give the meaning of the Latin phrase: *Ad mejorem dei gloriam.*
   Ans. To the greater glory of God

Geography

9. What term denotes lines on a map showing places of equal rainfall?
   Ans. Isohyets

Mathematics

10. What is 15% of 10% of 1500?
    Ans. $22\frac{1}{2}$

Theatre and Cinema

11. Who played the role of James Bond in the movie *Never Say Never Again*?
    Ans. Sean Connery

Bible Knowledge

12. Who was the Biblical mother of Issachar?
    Ans. Leah

Chemistry

13. In 1803, who discovered the atomic structure of matter?
    Ans. John Dalton

Mythology

14. In Norse mythology, what was the name of the wondrous ash-tree that was believed to support the universe?
    Ans. Yggdrasil

General Knowledge

15. Give one word which means "to start up a computer", "a type of shoe" and "to dismiss".
    Ans. Boot

Proverbs and Idioms

16. Give the meaning of the Jamaican proverb: "Hawse cyaan too gud fe carry him owna grass".
    Ans. No one should feel above assisting to secure that from which he will benefit.

History

17. In what century was the Bank of England formed: 16th, 17th or 18th?
    Ans. 17th

Art

18. Which artist is well-known for his work *Snow Storm: Steamboat off Harbour's Mouth*?
    Ans. J.M.W. Turner

Theatre and Cinema

19. Name the star of the movie *The Truman Show*.
    Ans. Jim Carrey

Geography

20. The Guyanese town of New Amsterdam stands at the mouth of which river?
    Ans. Berbice

Mathematics

21. If $x^2 - 3x + 2 = 0$, what are the two values of x?
    Ans. 1, 2

General Knowledge

22. Which city is known as the Athens of the North?
    Ans. Edinburgh

Foreign Languages

23. What is the meaning of the French verb *venir*?
    Ans. To come

Music

24. Which Jamaican entertainer was named Winston Rodney at birth?
    Ans. Burning Spear

Literature

25. In Shakespeare's *The Merchant of Venice*, with whom does Jessica elope, taking much of Shylock's wealth with her?
    Ans. Lorenzo

Jamaican Heritage

26. Which people in Jamaica celebrate the traditional festival of Hussay?
    Ans. East Indians

Chemistry

27. Name the two elements in the alloy known as Dentist's Amalgam.
    Ans. Mercury and copper

Foreign Languages

28. What is meant by the Spanish question *Que te parece*??
    Ans. What do you think?

Theatre and Cinema

29. Which actor played the role of Shane in the 1953 movie of the same name?
    Ans. Alan Ladd

Sports

30. Which two European teams did Diego Maradona represent in club football?
    Ans. Barcelona and Napoli

Jamaican Heritage

31. Give the name of the brother of Norman Manley who died in World War I.
    Ans. Roy Manley

Geography

32. In which parish of Jamaica would you find Mount Airy?
    Ans. Westmoreland

General Knowledge

33. With which country do you associate KLM Airlines?
    Ans. The Netherlands

Music

34. Which is the highest adult male voice?
    Ans. Alto

Literature

35. Who wrote the poem *The Eve of St. Agnes*?
    Ans. John Keats

Mathematics

36. What is the value of 113 to the base 4 in the denary system?
    Ans. 23

Physics

37. What is the speed of sound at sea level at 0 degrees centigrade in metres per second?
    Ans. 331.7 m/s

Religious Knowledge

38. Which is the Jewish day of Atonement?
    Ans. Yom Kippur

Foreign Languages

39. What is the French for the month of April?
    Ans. *Avril*

English Language

40. Complete the simile: "As bold as ..."
    Ans. "... brass, or as a lion."

Quiz No. 16

I. The Alternate Section

Bible Knowledge

1. At the occupation of Palestine, the tribe of Reuben, together with which tribe was allotted pastureland east of the Jordan?

    Ans. Gad

2. In 721 B.C., how many of the tribes of Israel were conquered and transported to Assyria?

    Ans. 10

Chemistry

3. What is the chemical formula for massicot?

    Ans. PbO

4. What is the chemical formula for phenol?

    Ans. C_6H_5OH

History

5. In what year did Tortuga begin as a refuge for cow-killers from Western Hispaniola?

    Ans. 1629

6. Which governor-general of all the French islands sent Le Vasseur to be Governor of Tortuga in 1640?

    Ans. De Poincy

Music

7. *Death and Transfiguration and Don Quixote* are musical pieces by which composer?

    Ans. Richard Strauss

8. *Symphonic Studies* and *Kinderscenen* are solo piano pieces by which composer?

    Ans. Schumann

General Knowledge

9. On which street in Kingston would you find the headquarters of the Jamaica Manufacturers Association?

    Ans. Duke Street

10. On which street in Kingston would you find the headquarters of the Jamaica Chamber of Commerce?

    Ans. East Parade

Mathematics

11. What is the sum of the interior angles of a regular polygon with 8 sides?

    Ans. 1080 degrees

12. What is the sum of the interior angles of a regular polygon with 5 sides?

    Ans. 540 degrees

Foreign Languages

13. Give the meaning of the French idiom *avoir le trac*.
    Ans. To be scared stiff

14. Give the meaning of the French idiom *tout a fait*.
    Ans. Quite; entirely

Geography

15. In which parish of Jamaica would you find Mammee Bay?
    Ans. St. Ann

16. In which African country would you find the Gemsbok National Park?
    Ans. Botswana

Chemistry

17. What colour is given by lithium in the flame test?
    Ans. Red

18. What colour is given by copper halides in the flame test?
    Ans. Blue

Jamaican Heritage

19. Name the island at the northern end of Long Bay, Negril, which was used for filming the South Sea scenes in *Twenty Thousand Leagues Under the Sea*.
    Ans. Booby Cay

20. Name the lighthouse near Port Maria, St. Mary, which helps to protect marine interests along Jamaica's east coast.
    Ans. Galina Point Lighthouse

Foreign Languages

21. What is the meaning of the Spanish: *Les debo quinientas pesetas*?
    Ans. I owe them 500 pesetas.

22. What is the meaning of the Spanish: *Deberia partir manana*?
    Ans. He should leave tomorrow.

History

23. Henry Morgan's first expedition in the Caribbean was against Puerto del Principe on which island?
    Ans. Cuba

24. Under which governor did Henry Morgan serve as Lieutenant-Governor in Jamaica?
    Ans. Lord Vaughan

Art

25. Which French artist painted *Le Bucheron*?
    Ans. Corot

26. Which French artist painted *Bois de Boulogne*?
    Ans. Dufy

Physics

27. What term in physics denotes the quantum of thermal energy in the lattice vibrations of a crystal?
    Ans. Phonon

28. If "f" is the vibrational frequency the magnitude of the phonon is "hf". What is denoted by "h"?
    Ans. Planck's constant

Foreign Languages

29. What is the meaning of the French verb *verser*?
    Ans. To pour

30. What is the meaning of the French verb *verifier*?
    Ans. To check

Literature

31. Who wrote the novel *The Conservationist*?
    Ans. Nadine Gordimer

32. Who wrote the novel *Schindler's Ark*?
    Ans. Thomas Kenneally

Proverbs and Idioms

33. Explain the Jamaican proverb "man ded, tree grow up to im doe mout'".
    Ans. What an individual would not tolerate in his lifetime can easily happen after he has passed away.

34. Explain the Jamaican proverb "craben cow alwaze tink nex nayba ghinny grass fatta".
    Ans. Persons not satisfied with what they have always regard other people as being more fortunate than themselves.

History

35. Which former governor of Virginia, a member of the Continental Congress, became Secretary of State in President Washington's cabinet?
    Ans. Thomas Jefferson

36. Which former senator from Massachusetts, who angered his fellow Federalists by supporting Jefferson's policies, was Secretary of State in President James Monroe's cabinet?
    Ans. John Quincy Adams

Physics

37. If pressure is 2 atmospheres, how much is this in Pascals?
    Ans. 2.026×10^5

38. What term denotes the rotating part of an electric motor or dynamo, consisting of coils of wire?
    Ans. Armature

Music

39. Who composed the ballet *The Firebird*?
    Ans. Igor Stravinsky

40. Who composed *Rhapsody on a Theme of Paganini*?
    Ans. Rachmaninov

II. The Speed Section

Speed Questions for Team A

1. Give one word which denotes the overhanging edge of a roof or thatch.
    Ans. Eaves

2. Which constant has the value 1.380622 x 10^{-23} J/K?
    Ans. Boltzman

3. What is the meaning of the Spanish *Que yo sepa*?
    Ans. As far as I know.

4. Which is the oldest sports club in the Commonwealth Caribbean?
    Ans. Kingston Cricket Club

5. Which Italian word, meaning literally flight, denotes in music a form of composition in which the basic principle is imitative counterpoint of several voices?
    Ans. Fugue

6. By which treaty, and in what year, did the French promise to stop buccaneering in return for Spanish recognition of St. Domingue?
    Ans. Ratisbon (1684)

7. Which territory did Kareem Streete-Thompson represent at the 1992 Olympic Games?
    Ans. Cayman Islands

8. What is the chemical formula for phosgene?
    Ans. $COCl_2$

9. Give the meaning of the French *trouver difficile de*.
    Ans. To find it difficult to

10. On which river is Quebec City located?
    Ans. The St. Lawrence River

11. Who composed the opera *The Damnation of Faust*?
    Ans. Berlioz

12. What term in physics denotes the type of radio transmission system in which the frequency of a carrier wave is modulated rather than its amplitude?
    Ans. Frequency modulation

13. Mount Kebnekaise is the highest point in which European country: Sweden or Austria?
    Ans. Sweden

14. Which Jamaican national hero was a notable schoolboy athlete?
    Ans. Norman Manley

15. What is the meaning of the Spanish *no cabe duda*?
    Ans. There is no doubt.

16. In which city were the Olympic Games held in 1904?
    Ans. St. Louis

17. Give an eight-letter word, beginning with "b" which means a temporary encampment without tents.
    Ans. Bivouac

18. Name the photosensitive cell in the retina of the eye which is essential for vision in dim light.
    Ans. Rods

19. Which team won the World Cup in cricket in 1987?
    Ans. Australia

20. Born at Figueras, this artist painted *Christ of St John of the Cross*, but he is best known for his *Persistence of Memory*. Name him.
    Ans. Salvador Dali

21. Whose novel, *The Old Devils*, won the Booker Prize in 1986?
    Ans. Kingsley Amis

22. Which Jamaican entertainer is referred to as the Don?
    Ans. Don Drummond

23. Explain the Jamaican proverb "siddung nebba seh gittup".
    Ans. When your environment is conducive to comfort and relaxation, it is very difficult to leave.

24. By which treaty did Surinam remain Dutch in exchange for New York, which became English?
    Ans. Treaty of Breda

25. To which phylum do starfish and relatives belong.
    Ans. Echinodermata

26. For what purpose would you use Kipp's apparatus in the laboratory?
    Ans. To produce a supply of any gas that can be evolved by the action of a liquid on a solid without heating.

27. Which city did Islamabad replace as the capital of Pakistan?
    Ans. Karachi

28. What is the meaning of the abbreviation JBA in Jamaica?
    Ans. Jamaica Bookmakers Association

29. Which two fluids combine with sperm to form semen?
    Ans. Seminal and prostatic fluids

30. Give the meaning of the Spanish verb *devolver*.
    Ans. To give back

31. Who invented the tape recorder?
    Ans. Valdemar Poulsen

32. According to legend, which Arawak Indian used her supernatural powers to change the course of the river which now bears her name?
    Ans. Martha Brae

33. Spell the word ACCESSIBLE.

34. Which country was formerly known as South West Africa?
    Ans. Namibia

35. What is the French for "the result"?
    Ans. *Le resultat*

36. Which artist painted *The Stonemason's Yard*?
    Ans. Canaletto

37. Which English sea captain claimed before Parliament, in 1738, that the Spanish had cut off his ear, giving rise to conflict between England and Spain.
    Ans. Captain Jenkins

38. What is the direction from Madagascar to the Seychelles?
    Ans. Northeast

39. What is the value of 222 to the base 5 in the denary system?
    Ans. 62

40. In Orwell's *Animal Farm*, what was the name of the original owner of the farm on which the animals revolted?
    Ans. Mr. Jones

Speed Questions for Team B

1. Give one word which denotes a right of way or similar right over another person's grounds, in law.
   Ans. Easement

2. Which physical property has the approximate value 1.675×10^{-27} kg?
   Ans. The rest mass of the neutron

3. What is the meaning of the Spanish los *conocio ayer*?
   Ans. He met them yesterday.

4. Which Jamaican governor was the first patron of the Kingston Cricket Club?
   Ans. Eyre

5. What is the general term for the group of low-pitched, valved brass wind instruments, including the sousaphone?
   Ans. Tuba

6. By which treaty of 1654 did the Dutch agree to accept English commercial regulations in the New World?
   Ans. Treaty of Westminster

7. Which former cricketer received the highest votes as the "best player of our time" in a poll by the Wisden Monthly at the end of the 20th century?
   Ans. Don Bradman

8. What is the chemical formula for phosphine?
   Ans. PH_3

9. Give the meaning of the French *prendre au serieux*.
   Ans. To take seriously

10. On which river is Madrid located?
    Ans. The Manzanares River

11. Who composed *The Faust Symphony*?
    Ans. Liszt

12. Which of Kepler's laws refers to the radius vector of each planet?
    Ans. The second

13. Erigavo is the highest point in which African country: Ghana or Somalia?
    Ans. Somalia

14. Which Jamaican national hero conducted businesses which included money-lending?
    Ans. Bustamante

15. What is the meaning of the Spanish *me hace falta una casa*?
    Ans. I need a house.

16. In which city were the Olympic Games held in 1928?
    Ans. Amsterdam

17. Give a seven-letter word, beginning with "p" which means self-important, magnificent, or splendid.
    Ans. Pompous

18. Name the pigment found in rods of the eye.
    Ans. Rhodopsin

19. Which team won the World Cup in cricket in 1975?
    Ans. West Indies

20. Born at Saragossa, this artist painted *Blind Guitarist*, but he is best known for *The Execution of the Rebels*. Name him.
    Ans. Goya

21. Whose novel, *The Remains of the Day*, won the Booker Prize in 1989?
    Ans. Kazuo Ishiguro

22. In which decade did Don Drummond join the Skatalites in Jamaica?
    Ans. 1960s

23. Explain the Jamaican proverb "chubble no set like rain".
    Ans. When trouble confronts us, there is usually no prior warning.

24. In the 17th century Caribbean, which were the two naval bases held by the British?
    Ans. English Harbour, Antigua, and Port Royal, Jamaica

25. To which phylum do jellyfish and relatives belong?
    Ans. Coelenterata

26. In a mercury cell, of what is the cathode made?
    Ans. Mercury (II) oxide mixed with graphite

27. Which city did Manilla replace as the capital of the Philippines?
    Ans. Quezon City

28. With which sport in Jamaica do you most associate Cecil Charlton?
    Ans. Horseracing

29. What is the name of the long duct into which sperm passes when it leaves the epididymis?
    Ans. Vas deferens

30. Give the meaning of the Spanish phrase *el sol se pone*?
    Ans. The sun sets.

31. Who invented the the tank?
    Ans. Ernest Swinton

32. In what decade in Jamaica did rafting begin on the Martha Brae River?
    Ans. 1970s

33. Spell the word POLYPODY.

34. Which country was formerly known as Aden?
    Ans. Yemen (Peoples Democratic Republic)

35. What is the French for "the problem"?
    Ans. *Le probleme*

36. Which artist painted *The Morning Walk*?
    Ans. Thomas Gainsborough

37. Who was the Prime Minister of England at the start of the War of Jenkins Ear?
    Ans. Robert Walpole

38. What is the direction from Kosovo to Belgrade?
    Ans. North

39. What is the value of 111 to the base five in the denary system?
    Ans. 31

40. In Orwell's *Animal Farm*, what was the original name of the farm on which the animals revolted?
    Ans. Manor Farm

III. The Signal Section

Mathematics

1. The universal set has 40 elements. Set J has 25 and set K has 30. What is the smallest number of elements in J union K?

    Ans. 30

Theatre and Cinema

2. Who performed the title song in the James Bond movie *Live and Let Die*?

    Ans. Paul McCartney and Wings

General Knowledge

3. Whose fifth postulate in mathematics states that one and only one line parallel to a given line can be drawn through a point external to the line?

    Ans. Euclid's

Jamaican Heritage

4. Which Jamaican port did Ella Wheeler Wilcox call "the most exquisite port on earth"?

    Ans. Port Antonio

Proverbs and Idioms

5. Explain the Jamaican proverb "lawn fe danse a yaad, befoe yu go abroad".

    Ans. Practice at home before going out in public to avoid embarrassing yourself by not doing something right.

Sports

6. Who holds the record for the highest individual score at the World Cup in cricket in a single match?

    Ans. Gary Kirsten

Foreign Languages

7. Give two Spanish verbs which mean "to end".

    Ans. *Terminar*; *acabar*

Music

8. What was the nationality of the composer Anton Bruckner?

    Ans. Austrian

Literature

9. Who wrote the novel *The English Patient*?

    Ans. Michael Ondaatje

History

10. In what year was the National Association for the Advancement of Coloured People established: 1910, 1950 or 1990?

    Ans. 1910

Chemistry

11. Which element has atomic number 21: lead, scandium or iron?

    Ans. Scandium

English Language

12. Give an eight-letter word beginning with "v" which means "word for word".

    Ans. Verbatim

History

13. Who was the English Prime Minister at the start of the Seven Years' War?

    Ans. William Pitt

Physics

14. What term in physics denotes the deflection of any radiation as a result of its interaction with matter?
    Ans. Scattering

Biology

15. How many species of toad are there in Jamaica?
    Ans. One

General Knowledge

16. What title, meaning viceroy, was given to rulers of Egypt in the period beginning in 1863?
    Ans. Khedive

Music

17. Who composed the orchestral piece On *Hearing the First Cuckoo in Spring*?
    Ans. Delius

English Language

18. Distinguish between the words "pillory" and "pillage".
    Ans. Pillory means a wooden framework with holes for the head and hands of an offender exposed to public ridicule (or to expose to ridicule); pillage means to plunder, especially as practised in war.

Physics

19. What term denotes photography in which a slow process is photographed by a series of single exposures on a cinematic film at regular intervals?
    Ans. Time lapse photography

Theatre and Cinema

20. Name the male star of the movie *Bridges of Madison County*.
    Ans. Clint Eastwood

Chemistry

21. What term, synonymous with neutron excess, is given by the difference between the number of neutrons in an isotope and the number of protons?
    Ans. Isotopic number

Mathematics

22. What is the smallest value of x if $\tan 3x = 1$?
    Ans. 15 degrees

Sports

23. Of the 3 Ws in West Indian cricket, which one became the captain of the West Indies cricket team?
    Ans. Frank Worrell

Local and International Affairs

24. Name the newspaper publisher who received the Order of Jamaica in 1998.
    Ans. Oliver Clarke

History

25. In what century did the cabinet-maker Thomas Chippendale live?
    Ans. 18th

Proverbs and Idioms

26. Complete the Jamaican proverb "Me owl but ..."
    Ans. "... me noh cowl."

Geography

27. What is the capital of Guinea-Bissau?
    Ans. Bissau

General Knowledge

28. In which country did the poinsettia originate?
    Ans. Mexico

Physics

29. What is the kinetic energy of a body of mass 10 gm moving at 0.4 m/s?
    Ans. 0.008 J

Art

30. Which artist painted *Marriage a la Mode*?
    Ans. Hogarth

Foreign Languages

31. What is the occupation of *le mecanicien navigant* in France?
    Ans. The navigator

Music

32. Give the name of the group which Smokey Robinson once led.
    Ans. The Miracles

General Knowledge

33. Give the names of the two space missions in which John Glenn has travelled to space?
    Ans. Friendship 7 and Discovery

Chemistry

34. What is the IUPAC name for urea?
    Ans. Carbamide

Biology

35. Which hormone is abbreviated as TSH?
    Ans. Thyroid-stimulating hormone

Mythology

36. In mythology, who was the father of Tantalus?
    Ans. Zeus

Mathematics

37. What is the area of a trapezium with parallel sides of length 8 and 12 cm, and perpendicular distance 3 cm?
    Ans. 30 sq. cm

Bible Knowledge

38. What did Jesus answer when the Jews asked him if he had seen Abraham?
    Ans. "Before Abraham was, I am"

Geography

39. The Don Figueroa, May Day and Carpenter Mountains pass through which Jamaican parish?
    Ans. Manchester

Jamaican Heritage

40. At the time of formation of which Jamaican parish were settlers there entitled to two barrels of beef and one of flour?
    Ans. Portland

Bibliography

Allison, Wick, *That's in the Bible* (Dell Publishing)(1994).

Augier, F.R., S.C. Gordon, D.G. Hall and M. Reckord, *The Making of the West Indies* (Longman Caribbean) (1967).

Barton, John G., (Compilation), *Progressive Brain Teasing Quizzes* (Elliot Right Way Books)(1990).

Bent, R.M., and Enid Bent-Golding, *A Complete Geography of Jamaica* (Collins)(1966).

Best, Wilfred D., *The Students' Companion: Caribbean Edition* (Longman Caribbean)(1991).

Biggs, John, and Peter Simpson, *Multiple Choice Questions in Advanced Level Chemistry* (Cambridge University Press)(1985).

Black, Clinton V., *History of Jamaica* (Longman Caribbean)(1983 edition).

Black, Clinton V., *Jamaica Guide* (William Collins & Sangster (Jamaica) Ltd (First Edition, 1973).

Bolton, W., *Multiple Choice Questions for A-Level Physics* (Heinemann Educational Books)(1987).

Campbell, Alvin, and Louis Marriot, *Gold Rush Jamaican Style: Jamaica in World Athletics 1948–92* (Louis Marriot)(1992).

Carlinsky, Dan, *The Complete Bible Quiz Book* (Wings Books)(1985).

Clive Carpenter (ed.), *The Guinness Book of Answers: The Complete Reference Handbook* (10th ed., 1995).

Cleveland, Ceil, *Who, What, When, Where, Why, In the World of Literature* (Barron's Educational Series, Inc.)(1991).

Clugson, M.J., (ed.), *The New Penguin Dictionary of Science* (Penguin Books)(1998).

Cross, Wilber, *Who, What, When, Where, Why, In the World of Geography* (Barron's Educational Series, Inc.)(1991).

Crystal, David, *The Cambridge Factfinder* (Cambridge University Press)(Updated ed., 1994).

Deeson, E., *Physics: Basic Facts* (Harper Collins Publishers)(3rd ed., 1991).

Dempsey, Michael W. (ed.), *New Horizon Factfinder* (Parragon, 1993).

Downes, P.J., and E.A. Griffith, *Le Francais d'Aujourd'hui, Troisieme Partie* (Hodder and Stoughton)(1968).

Dyde, Brian, *Caribbean Companion, The A to Z Reference* (Macmillan Education Ltd.)(1992).

Encyclopaedia Britannica Inc., *The New Encyclopaedia Britannica*, Volumes 1 to 29 (Encyclopaedia Britannica, Inc.) (15th ed., 1994).

Folkes, Marlene, *Nelson CXC Practice Tests: Maths* (Nelson Caribbean) (Revised ed., 1988).

Franck, Irene M., *On the Tip of Your Tongue* (Penguin Group)(1990).

Gleaner Company, The, *The Daily Gleaner* (various dates).

Gleaner, The Sunday, (various dates).

Gleaner Company, The, *The Gleaner, Geography and History of Jamaica* (24th ed., 1995).

Gleaner Company, The, *Chemistry, Revision Text for G.C.E./CXC & Related O'Level Examinations* (not dated).

Griffith, Benjamin, *Who, What, When, Where, Why, In the World of Music and Art* (Barron's Educational Series, Inc.)(1991).

Hirsch, E.D., Jr., Joseph F. Kett, James Trefil, *The Dictionary of Cultural Literacy* (Houghton Mifflin Company)(2nd ed., 1993).

Hewett, R.P. Hewett (ed.), *A Choice of Poets* (Nelson)(1989 edition).

Jace and Cokerill, *Bumper Quiz Book* (Clarion)(1995).

Jackson, Barry, and Peter Whiteley, *Longman CXC Physics* (Longman Caribbean)(1996).

Jamaica Observer Ltd., The, *The Daily Observer* (various dates). *The Weekend Observer* (various dates).

Jones, Philip, *Nelson CXC Practice Tests: Integrated Science* (Nelson Caribbean)(1987).

Lass, Abraham H., David Kiremidjian and Ruth M. Goldstein, *The Facts on File Dictionary of Classical, Biblical and Literary Allusions* (Facts on File Publications)(1987).

Louis, David, *2201 Fascinating Facts* (The Ridge Press) (1983).

Maciver, Angus, *Concise First Aid in English* (Robert Gibson & Sons (Glasgow) Ltd.) (1984).

McKenzie, A.E.E., *Physics* (Cambridge University Press) (1970).

McMonagle, D. (ed.), *Science: Basic Facts* (Harper Collins)(2nd ed., 1992).

Mahase, Compton, *CXC Revision for Chemistry* (Cambridge University Press)(1988).

Manley, Michael, *A History of West Indies Cricket* (Andre Deutsch)(1988).

Mannion, K., J. Potter, K. Stuart, *The Students' Companion Practice Book* (Longman Caribbean)(1986).

Martin, John G., *Increase Your Vocabulary* (Prentice-Hall Inc.)(1967).

Martinson, Thomas H., and Juliana Fazzone, *Supercourse for College Board Achievement Tests* (Arco, Prentice Hall)(1991).

Mitchelmore, June, *Nelson CXC Practice Tests: Biology* (Nelson Caribbean)(1986).

Morris-Brown, Vivien, *The Jamaica Handbook of Proverbs* (Island Heart Publishers)(1993).

Murphy, Hilary, *Hutchinson's Pocket Quiz Book* (Helicon Publishing) (1993).

Murray, R.N., *Nelson's West Indian History* (Nelson)(1971).

Oblitas, M.M.L., *'A' Level Multiple Choice Questions: Physical Chemistry* (Oliver & Boyd)(1971).

Raimes, James, *The Columbia Quiz Book* (Columbia University Press)(1993).

Ramchand, Kenneth, *West Indian Narrative: An Introductory Anthology* (Nelson Caribbean)(Revised ed., 1980).

Ramchand, Kenneth, *The West Indian Novel and its Background* (Faber and Faber) (1970).

Robinson, Carey, *Fight for Freedom: The Destruction of Slavery in Jamaica* (Kingston Publishers Limited)(2nd ed., 1993).

Scarr, J.R., *Present Day Spanish*, Volume II (Thomas Nelson and Sons Ltd.) (1991).

Scott, W.A.H., *Chemistry: Basic Facts* (Harper Collins Publishers) (3rd ed., 1991).

Selectco Publications, *The Jamaica Directory of Personalities 2001–2002* (Selectco Publications Ltd.)(2002).

Senior, Olive, *A–Z of Jamaican Heritage* (Heinemann Educational Books (Caribbean) Limited, The Gleaner Company)(1987 edition).

Smith, John, *How to Win any Pub Quiz* (Guinness Publishing) (1993).

Smith, William, *A Dictionary of the Bible* (Thomas Nelson Publishers)(1986).

Strouf, Judie L.H., *Literature Lover's Book of Lists* (Prentice Hall Press)(1998).

Taylor, Boswell (Compilation) *BBC Top of the Form Quiz Book 1* (Knight Books, Hodder and Stoughton)(1980).

Thackrah, J.R., and R.F. Stapley, *Twentieth Century History: Basic Facts* (Harper Collins)(2nd ed., 1993).

Walker, S.H., *C.X.C. and G.C.E. Multiple Choice Math Samples (Metric)* (JAG Clarke Co. Ltd.)(1993).

Walmsley, Ann (Compilation), *The Sun's Eye: West Indian Writing for Young Readers* (Longman Caribbean)(New Edition, 1989).

Watson, G. Llewellyn, *Jamaican Sayings, With Notes on Folklore, Aesthetics and Social Control* (Florida A & M University Press/ Tallahassee)(1991).

Williams, Eric, *From Columbus to Castro: The History of the Caribbean, 1492–1969* (Vintage Books)(1984 ed.).

Williams, Geoffrey, *Portrait of World History* (Edward Arnold (Publishers) Ltd.)(1962).

Worth, Fred, *The Trivia Encyclopedia* (Brooke House)(1974).

Zahler, Diane, and Kathy A. Zahler, *Test Your Cultural Literacy* (Prentice Hall)(2nd ed., 1993).

www.ingramcontent.com/pod-product-compliance
Lightning Source LLC
Chambersburg PA
CBHW081152270326
41930CB00014B/3132